AF236010

1

Hebrew Astrology

*… according to
the Writings and Speeches of
Friedrich Weinreb*

(His Memory for a Blessing)

Bibliografische Information der Deutschen Nationalbibliothek: Die Deutsche Nationalbibliothek verzeichnet diese Publikation in der Deutschen Nationalbibliografie; detaillierte bibliografische Daten sind im Internet über dnb.dnb.de abrufbar.

© 2020 Janosch Moser (Jochanan Massorah)
Herstellung und Verlag: BoD – Books on Demand, Norderstedt

ISBN: 978-3-7526-4230-8

Der gesamte Text dieses Buches ist auch frei verfügbar zu finden unter LaThalmidim.net

Preface

The particular motivation for this author (of German mother tongue) to write a book about Hebrew Astrology in the English language – would be stuff for an own book. So let us skip that. Just: may all the grammar mistakes and all strange choices of expression be forgiven. Someone really interested in, thoroughly fascinated by the topic, will certainly be able to understand everything anyways.

Helpful for the consumption by the reader will be a basic knowledge about major biblical topics – but for the beginning such knowledge is not even necessarily required in all depths. All Bible scriptures spoken about during the text will generally be given in brackets or similarily, so the reader may read the respective story or single verse at that point of his reading to increase his understanding. Nevertheless a basic knowledge of the greatest Bible-narratives is recommended beforehand, because the very fundamentals cannot be introduced to the reader purely by this little book (for instance the Creation account, the Exodus out of Egypt, Jesus' life, death and resurrection, etc.).

A few words regarding the sources for the content of this book: The Chassidic-Jewish writer and speaker (or ‚preacher') Friedrich Weinreb (may his memory be for a blessing) is by far the main source of all the following information.

Indeed, originally this project was intended to only summarize one specific book of Weinreb (named ‚Die Astrologie in der Jüdischen Mystik' in its German original, based on a series of speeches by

Weinreb) which is elaborating on this Astrology-topic – but then … the planned 'summary' got even longer than the book to be summarized itself …

Beside this specific Weinreb-book and some others of his writings and speeches, sources for the presented material are especially the Holy Bible itself and the Jewish tradition, the so-called 'Oral Thora' (which nonetheless is written down by now to a very high degree; most famously the 'Talmud' and several compositions of 'Midrashim', as well as countless Commentaries on these things from different ages and perspectives).

The sources could be called 'Kabbalah' in the broadest sense – Only this term is so heavily distorted in its usage of modern times, that one probably should be careful with using it nowadays to describe something serious …

The book is structured only roughly in seven chapters or 'parts'. The table of contents will name them and give some key words of each part, similar as it is common practice in especially those of Weinreb's books which are based on oral lessons he gave.

Last but not least, it shall be mentioned that the writing of this book only became possible thanks to the fecund work of the *Friedrich-Weinreb-Stiftung* ('Friedrich Weinreb Foundation') in Zurich. Without their translating of many of Weinreb's originally dutch-language wiritings and speeches into the German (and sometimes into the English) language, without their writing down of so many, many hours of oral lessons Weinreb gave during his lifetime, and without their final publishing and presenting of all

6

these great words – there would have been only very, very little chance to know about most of it at all. So blessed be everyone supporting this Foundation!

And may the Heavens now also bless the experience of this little book! The author at least is feeling already blessed, just by having been confronted with these contents in his life here on Earth. So may it be the same blessing for all true seekers!

In infinite Gratefulness to the Eternal God,

Jochanan Massorah

Frankfurt am Main, Eighth of August 2018

*****

Preface to the second edition

After the first edition of this book, which has been only a private print of 26 pieces in 2019, now it has been decided that there should be another edition of the text. This time as an actual publication (i. e. with ISBN), via 'Books on Demand'. Unfortunately the text itself could not be corrected concerning the numerous typos and grammar flaws. But the lack of English language publications on the works of Friedrich Weinreb has led the author to the conclusion, that a publication even of the uncorrected text nevertheless would be imperative.

Special thanks shall be expressed to the *Weinreb-Tonarchiv* (weinreb-tonarchiv.de) and to the man who is in charge of it, Dieter Miunske. He only is able to offer this great gift to Humankind, because there are people who support him financially by deliberate donations. So please consider supporting him, too!!

May the Great Work ever continue ...

Jochanan Massorah

Frankfurt am Main, 19th of October 2020

Table of Contents

9

Horoscope; 8, 9 and 10 as the ,Planets of Hope';
True Prophetic Vision and the 11th and 12th Planet;
Yom Kippur Katan; Story of the Day Labourers;
,Israel is living above the Stars'.

7. Part: The Wise One and the Serpent at his Daughter's Wedding ... p. 207

The Wise Man Aqiba; Meeting his First Wife; Aqiba's Years of Learning; The Beautiful Roman Woman as the Second Wife; Journey to Paradise; 4 Stages of the Journey; Aqiba's 3 Companions; Kabbalah's Perspective on the Journey; The Wedding of Aqiba's Daughter; Aqiba's Babylonian Friend, the Star Gazer; Aqiba's Explanation of the True Horoscope for his Daughter.

The Basics; Astrology of the ‚Babylonians' vs ‚Hebrew Astrology'

In this first section of the introduction to the ‚Astrology of the Hebrews', how it is described especially by Friedrich Weinreb, it is necessary to lay a fundament of some basic concepts of what can be called ‚Ancient Wisdom'. This ‚wisdom' is not at all limited to the so-called ‚Hebrews' as one distinct people of human history, but it is found to a lesser or larger degree in many, if not all of the ancient cultures of Mankind.

Here the word ‚ancient' does not necessarily mean actually ‚far away in past times', but rather something like ‚far deep down in the human sub- or unconsciousness' (that area where all the ‚myths' flow from …). That is, true ‚Ancient Wisdom' is a form of knowledge, which is present in every human being, but normally has to be ‚digged out' first nowadays, before it can be experienced consciously, because the modern world tends to work directly against it with all their fixation on one-sided rationality and purely causal explanation for developments in the measurable realm.

The word ‚Hebrew', too, needs to be clarified first. It is not in the first place referring to a specific ethnic group, but rather to something like a 'spiritual community', present throughout all times, and especially the word refers to a layer of being, too, which is present in every single individual: that layer in all of us, which stems ‚from the Other Side'. Although of course historically the ‚Hebrew element' indeed is manifest for a certain period of time as an actual ethnic group; but already ‚back then' this

12

group has been always open for everyone, who follows the eternal principals, too (see for example Exodus 12, 49; Numeri 15, 14-15).

Two variants of Astrology, which are seen as being opposed to each other to a certain degree, can be called ‚the Astrology of Becoming‘ and ‚the Astrology of Being‘. The ladder will be the main topic of this introduction, while the former is the one widely (more or less) known to the modern world, in the shape of daily newspaper horoscopes and of the deeper ‚esoteric‘ treatment of the zodiacal signs.

That wider known ‚Astrology of Becoming‘ is called the ‚Babylonian Astrology‘ from the point of view of this ‚Other Astrology‘, the one of ‚Being‘, the ‚Hebrew one‘.

From the Hebrew language, the name ‚Babylon‘ is pronounced ‚Babel‘ (written with the three consonant letters B-B-L) and can be translated as ‚confusion; mixture, intermingling‘. It is one symbol for ‚this chaotic world we live in‘, wherein no boundaries are kept forever and where everything flows into each other; but it is nonetheless a ‚world of organization‘, too, for in the ‚area of Babel‘ it happened according to the Bible (see Genesis 11), that Mankind united for the first time and started their unholy work on the so-called ‚Tower of Babel‘, an everlasting project, by which we human beings are trying (until nowadays) to ‚reach heaven‘, and by this: control the spread of human population, hold the whole world together by our OWN rules and ‚make ourselves a name before the Gods‘.

According to these characteristics of the mythical

13

‚Babel', the ‚Babylonian Astrology' has certain characteristics itself: It is called the ‚female' astrology; that means, this astrology is (almost) only looking at the ‚appearing', at ‚this side of the world', at the concrete, at the observable and measureable, it is a system completely based on causality; it is first and for all ‚calculating', searching for ‚perfect', definite results. By this it is quite ‚unfree', because according to its understanding of reality everything is (and always stays) fixed into a network of force and necessity, intermingled with everything else. That brings with it, that there is no real individuality of the single individuals, whose ‚horoscopes' are looked at, because only the observable 'star constellations' (or in a more modern understanding: the ‚measurable factors' in one's life, like the ‚genes', or the ‚epigenetics' being determined by the environment and the way of being raised in this environment, and the happenings of one's life) are determining the whole destiny. WHO it is, what inner quality that human being uniquely brings into this world from out of his/her Source on the Other Side, does not really matter for this kind of Astrology. Nevertheless, this Babylonian Astrology indeed IS quite correct, from a purely causal look at reality.

But the OTHER Astrology, which shall be presented in the following, is the ‚Hebrew' one, the ‚Astrology of Being', not of ‚Becoming'. The word ‚Hebrew' comes from the hebrew word ‚Eber' (written with the consonant letters E-B-R), which can be translated with a wide spectrum of meanings, including ‚transitory'; ‚one, who transcends'; ‚one, from the other side' and similar.

14

This ‚Hebrew Astrology' thus is the ‚Astrology of the Eternal', the one looking for ‚the Other Side', too, and by this it is including the single individuals deliberate influence on his/her own destiny. This is expressed in the mythical language as counting with the so-called ‚hidden planets', too. Those ‚hidden planets' are not observable in the outside world, but only are traceable through the individuals uniqueness. And especially these ‚hidden planets' can always make the decisive difference (far reaching into this world of causality, too!) …

Some basic concepts of the Ancient Wisdom have to be established first, before it can be spoken of the actual Astrology. Namely the three principles we can call: the ‚Male-Female-Antagonism bearing the Fruit $(3^2+4^2=5^2)'$, the ‚2-to-1-Journey of Creation through Mankind' and the ‚1-4-Principle as the inner structure of salvation, i.e. of the looking through the manifold, seeing the hidden unity of the manifold' (and by this, realizing this Unity of the ‚Four' as being of another level of reality, not out of the ‚Four' itself). Without further explanations these three names cannot really be understood of course, because they use a type of ‚language' or wording, which is very uncommon in our society.

All of these principles are to a large part expressed in terms of 'numbers' and their relations to each other. This is, because in the Ancient Wisdom the numbers are understood rather as ‚values', than as mere ‚digits', it is looked firstly at their ‚quality' instead of purely looking at the logical ‚quantity' of those numbers, as we do it nowadays, only using numbers as tools to organize reality for our everyday-purposes.

On the first view it may seem to be complicated, if one is not familiar with this way of thinking. But as soon as one gets accustomed to the way of speech and to the fundamental Biblical symbolisms, it simplifies things very heavily and opens the view for broader connections and correlations within the whole of creation, including oneself and one's relation to the surrounding world and concerning the happenings of one's (even everyday-)life.

Those aforementioned three fundamental principles now can be explained as being connected to what is called the ‚6th, 7th and 8th Day of Creation'. For this purpose it is necessary here to give a very short overview of the Biblical ‚Seven-Day-Work of Creation' in its schematic essence, how Friedrich Weinreb points it out in much more depth in his basic work ‚Roots of the Bible' (‚Schöpfung im Wort' in German).

So only very briefly: The 7 ‚days' (or 'stages') of Creation are grouped in 6+1 (the six days of ‚work', and the 7th being set apart, as the one day, where the Creator ‚is resting', representing this measurable ‚world of linear time' that we now live in as Mankind). And the ‚6 days of work' again are split in 2 x 3. These ‚two times three' means, that the second 3 days can be recognized as a mere repetition of the first 3 days, only on a new, a ‚higher' level. Thus it is a ‚duality of triads', from which that ‚6', as the ‚abstract basic pattern of creation', is built (and by the way, the ‚unfolding' of the number 3, which represents the ‚male', i.e. the ‚abstract' of this world, is the 6: 3+2+1=6).

Now: in each of the two 3-day-periods we firstly find the number 4 as the value of the actual ‚outer‘ actions of that period, since it is always 3 ‚days‘ being ‚built‘ out of 4 ‚words‘ (that is ‚actions‘) of God. Only on the final sixth day there are actually two additional ‚words‘ of God, which then sum up (with the 8 before) to 10 ‚God-actions‘ in total, which thus make the ‚concrete, experienceable scenery of creation‘ (and by the way again: the 10 is the ‚unfolding‘ of the number 4, which represents the ‚female‘, i.e. the ‚concrete‘ of this world: 4+3+2+1=10).

The ‚fulfillment‘ of a number (mathematically called its ‚potency‘) in this Ancient Wisdom then means the totality of combinations, in which the ‚containing‘ numbers can be put one next to another: 2 has as its potency 4 (2 x 2), because the only numbers contained by the 2 are the numbers 1 and 2, and those can be placed next to each other as 1×1, 1×2, 2×1, 2×2. Thus, 4 is the ‚fulfillment‘ of the 2. By this understanding it is said that: 4 (the number of the ‚female principle‘) is spiritually ‚the highest number‘ in our ‚World of Duality‘, so the 4 (respectively her derivatives, like the 40 and the 400) is the natural ’symbol of infinity‘, of ‚the whole‘ of any dualistic reality.

With that basic scheme sketched out, we can now look at the decisive three ‚days‘: the 6th , 7th and the coming 8th.

The ‚Sixth Day‘: On the 6th day of the mythical ‚creation week‘ Mankind is created. In the land of (mythical) ‚Egypt‘, later in the Biblical story, ‚Israel‘

17

then becomes a nation, developing out of the few descendants of Jacob (whose second name becomes ‚Israel‘ during his ’struggle with something spiritual‘; for details see Genesis 32, 24-31). And at the end of the 6th day of the creation week Mankind leaves ‚the Garden Eden‘, the ‚Paradise‘ (which is not anymore enjoyable for Mankind, after the ‚forbidden fruit‘ has ‚opened their eyes‘ and has shown them their own ’nakedness‘); just like Israel leaves the (until recently seemingly ‚well-functioning‘) land of Egypt (after they realized, how enslaved they actually are by Pharao and his world of ‚building‘, of unlimited material development). So, in the creation week, Mankind is created firstly in the ‚womb‘ (the ‚paradise‘) of Mother Earth and then born into the outer world of actual matter and time on the 6th day. And in the Hebrew tradition the liberation out of Egypt is basically compared to the birth-process of a child (with the ‚plagues‘ over Egypt understood as ‚labour pains‘ of the birthing mother; the people of Israel being ‚born out of Egypt‘ as ‚the firstborn Child of the Eternal‘).

With all these parallels it is reasonable to see ‚Egypt‘ as a furtherly unfolded symbol for the ‚6th Day‘ of Creation, where now the original Duality of that sixth day of Creation for the first time is being developed ‚to the broadest extent‘ (the ‚400 years of enslavement in Egypt‘), before then the liberation OUT OF this Duality, back to the ‚Oneness‘, can be experienced.

So the 6th Day represents the infinite ‚Split‘; the formation and/or sustainment of a World of Duality: the primeval Male-Female-Antagonism – but already containing the potential ‚Fruit' coming thereof (because from the beginning on there IS a prophecy of God, that there will be salvation nevertheless, namely the 'seed of the woman', which is going to be ‚crushing the serpents head'; see Genesis 3, 15) … In the creation week it was the first split of Mankind in Man and Woman, then the leaving of the ‚Paradise' to experience this duality on every level, the beginning of the actual ‚World of Duality' away from the Oneness with the Creator in the ‚Paradise'. And in Egypt later it is the already fully developed World of Duality, and with that full development of the split, it is the point now, where the ‚turn' has to happen, to bring everything back to its Source, to the ‚One' (and therefore the ‚redeemer' Moses is born, as a heavenly response to the lamenting and moaning of the children of Israel about their enslavement).

That antagonism ‚Male-Female' means many things in this traditional understanding of the fundamental dualism of all Creation: Invisible-Visible, Secret-Revelation, Abstract-Concrete, ‚Fire-Water', Day-Night, Light-Darkness, ‚Sun-Moon', Eternity-Time, Heaven and Earth, Creator and His (Act of) Creation. And much more.

And to make clear that there is not one of the two ‚being superior to the other', it can be looked for instance at the relation of fire and water in nature: If the fire is exceeding, it condenses the water ‚away' by its heat. But if the water is exceeding, it extincts the fire, suffocating it. So the two are just two extremes, each with its own strenght and weakness, depending on circumstances, not one in itself 'superiour' to the other.

By the way: In the Hebrew the word for ‚Heaven‘ ('sh'mayim') can be understood as the combination of the letter ‚Sh(in)‘, which is originally written in the form of a fire flame, and the word ‚Mayim‘, which means ‚water‘. So in the word ‚Sh'mayim‘ there is both united in Oneness, fire and water building one single entity, an equilibrium, which down here on material Earth cannot be present in the same harmonic way. That is, ‚in Heaven‘ there is always BOTH present in perfect harmony: Eternity AND Time, the Creator AND His Creation.

And that, what comes out of the ‚conversation‘ between ‚water and fire‘ here on Earth, between female and male, is the ‚Child‘, or the ‚Fruit‘: the result of the combination of the two extremes, but not just as the 'sum', like two numbers adding up, but as something completely new, which combines characteristics of the two ‚parents‘ in a unique way, never predictable from the human point of view, but always still detectable as stemming from these parents as the ‚fruit‘ of their coming together. Like 3+4 does not equal 5, but only the fulfillment of the 3 coming together with the fulfillment of the 4, so the fulfillment of both, the Male and the Female, equals the fulfillment of the 5, the Fruit, the Child $(3^2+4^2=5^2)$.

In a way, Mankind itself can be understood as the ‚Fruit‘ of the coming together of Heaven and Earth: Mankind ‚in the image and resemblance of God‘, where the Creator has come down INTO His own Creation, to bring the whole world in her diversity and manifoldness all back to the Source THROUGH this Mankind, where the Divine Breath has been

,blewn into the nose' of that ,Earth-taken' Human Being to make this Human Being an actual ,Living Soul' by this (see Genesis 2, 7), uniting Heaven and Earth.

The ,Seventh day': The 7th day of the Biblical Creation represents OUR world of time and space, the stage ,when God rests from his work', because ,everything is very good' (see Genesis 1, 31; 2, 2). That ,everything is very good' in our world is something, we human beings have our problems with to accept … But for the purpose of this world, she indeed is ,very good': this world with all her evil and struggle, death and diseases, won't ever let us come to a final rest, always drives us further, so that we never can think, we are ,finish' already. This world reminds us by her way of being, that it is the everlasting purpose of whole creation (after being created out of the Oneness of God, then splitting into the manifold): to get united again in the perception of Mankind (,in the image of God'), and this Mankind is functioning for that purpose as a (potential) Oneness vis-a-vis to the manifoldness of creation, of nature. And that means, every single human being is ,tying back' the whole world, which he or she perceives, out of the manifold forms of nature and culture into the oneness of the Source, which is always present deep down within him/her. Or the same said in simple numeric symbolism: ,bringing the created world back from the 2 to the 1'.

This whole journey through the worlds is represented by ,the 6th, 7th and 8th day of Creation', with the Eighth Day as the ,Coming World', the promised re-established Oneness of the origin, but now with the

21

experience of having been split into the manifoldness and having been reunited again, out of free will to connect back with the Oneness as our Source, with God, our Heavenly Father.

… and now, when we have established ‚Egypt‘ as the equivalent to the 6th day, and ‚getting liberated out of it by Moses‘ as the transition to the 7th day, then biblically we are coming into the ‚Wilderness/Desert‘ as the equivalent of that 7th day, wandering through this inhospitable world (content of the biblical books of Exodus, Leviticus, Numeri and Deuteronomy) until we are finally reaching the ‚8th day‘, the ‚Promised Land‘ Canaan/Israel (content of the biblical book of ‚Joshua‘, or in Hebrew ‚Yehoshua‘, the exact same name as the greek variant ‚Jesus‘ in the New Testament, meaning ‚Assistance of the Eternal‘).

This Promised Land is called ‚Canaan‘, as long as we still have not reached and conquered it, because it is still occupied by the ‚canaanites‘, the earlier inhabitants. And the word ‚canaan(ites)‘ is translateable as ‚business men; traders‘ … The land is only later called ‚Israel‘, when all the ‚traders‘, i.e. all the counting, calculating and business-doing, that purely rational and causal try to cope with reality, that constant looking for the personal benefit and so on, is ultimately erased and driven out from it …

The ‚Eighth Day‘: In the coming world of the so-called ‚8th Day‘ Mankind's reality is finally 'seen through' and understood, by means of the ‚1-4-principle‘, which explains the necessity of so-called ‚evil‘ in this world. The ‚1-4-principle‘ says, that ‚the

22

Five (= the FRUIT) is not built up of 5 equal ‚Ones‘, but it is built up of one ONE and of the FOUR in opposition to this One‘. And only by this specific structure the divine ‚One‘ becomes ‚consumable, useful, enjoyable‘ as such for Mankind in this ‚World of the Four‘.

Some examples in nature are: human body (1 head, 4 extremities), human hand (1 thumb, 4 fingers), air (1 part oxygen, 4 parts nitrogen), breathing-heartbeat-relation (1 breath while 4 heartbeats)

And some examples in Scripture are: two trees in the Garden Eden (Tree of Life with the numeric value of 233 and Tree of Knowledge of Good and Evil with the numeric value of 932, so a relation of 233 to 932, that is 1 to 4; Genesis 2,9); one river out of the Garden splitting into 4 streams ’nourishing the whole Earth‘ (Genesis 2,10); Jacob (also called ‚Israel‘, Archfather of the people of Israel) and his 4 wifes Lea, Rahel, Zilpah and Bilhah (see for example Genesis 35, 23-26); Joseph as king of Egypt collecting 1 fifth part of all the countries harvest for the coming seven ‚poor‘ years, while 4 fifth parts remain for the everyday-usage in the common ‚good‘ years until then (Genesis 41,34);

We see in these examples, that although it is always the ‚One‘, which makes the decisive effect, this ‚One‘ alone would not be sufficient in ‚this World of the 4‘: a hand without the four fingers, only with a thumb, would be quite useless; but if the thumb would be just like the other four fingers, the hand would be only an animal’s pawn. Similarly the oxygen of our air could not be breathed in without the 4 parts of nitrogen; or in the biblical symbolisms.

23

similarly the Archfather Israel without his 4 wifes would have been not the Archfather of the specific people of Israel developing out of his 12 sons (but the 4 wifes without their shared one husband would not have become the mothers of the people of Israel either). And similarly the ‚Tree of Life' in the Garden Eden would not have been an object of free decision for Mankind, to take (only) off ITS fruits, if there would not have been the other tree as temptation, the ‚forbidden one' of ‚knowledge of Good and Evil', as the ‚4 coming with the 1'. And by the way, if Mankind would have NEVER taken from the ‚forbidden fruit', i.e. from ‚the 4' … well, then the whole biblical story would have been veeeeery short and boring, right …

On this fundament now (the knowledge of the human ‚path through the desert' of this seventh day, from the sixth to the eighth: ‚bearing the fruit out of the convergence of male and female, to experience that fruit as the 5', by this experience the ‚coming from the 2 $[3^2+4^2]$ to the 1 $[=5^2]$', to finally be ‚honoring the ONE above – but not WITHOUT – the Four') appears the whole ‚Hebrew Astrology'.

The individual human being is now looked at as a continuum of two souls, a continuum pervading essentially the whole distance between earth and heaven (or 'sky', 'space', the realm of the stars and planets), namely the continuum of the 'neshamah' and the 'nephesh', translateable roughly as the ‚divine soul' and the ‚animal soul'. The actual human body of ‚flesh and blood' is merely the appearence of that duality of souls in this material world, the ‚female' (= visible, concrete) aspect of the human

24

being so to speak, while the soul-complex itself is the ,male' (= inwardly, abstract), the hidden aspect of every human being.

Now the ,divine soul' is said to be in constant contact with the Divine in Heaven, while the ,animal soul' is what is attached to our sensations and bodily feelings and thoughts of our heart.

And then there is something, which is called the ,ruach' (translated mostly as 'spirit'), that mediates between the ,divine soul' up there and the ,animal soul' down here. But this word ,ruach' is not only translateable as 'spirit'; it equally means ,wind, air', and beside this even ,direction; movement'. And the 12 zodiacal signs are accordingly the 12 ,directions and movements of the spirit' all around us, influencing the individual human being in 12 distinct qualities, connecting the individuals two soul-parts together throughout space.

Different as in the ,babylonian' system, in Hebrew Astrology the 12 zodiacal signs are divided into 3 groups, not into 4 (according to the ,4 Elements' Earth/Solid, Water/Liquid, Wind/Gaseous, Fire/Heat): 4 ,female' (or ,concrete') signs, 3 ,male' (or ,abstract') signs, 5 ,fruit'/'child' signs.

The female is envisioned as a ,horizontal' reality, male as a ,vertical' reality; and the fruit or child is envisioned consequently as the ,hypothenusis', completing the male and the female lines to a triangle; compare again to the famous ,Pythagorean Theorem', $3^2+4^2=5^2$.

One should be clear: every human being has ALL the zodiacal signs inside him-/herself, only some of the signs are more prominent, others are less prominent; depending on the movements of the ‚planets‘ throughout the zodiacal signs (and not ONLY at the time of birth, although that specific point in time HAS a certain weight of course).

Planets are generally the ‚moving‘ aspects, which are moving on the background of the (relatively) steady, enduring star-pictures of the Zodiac. In the Hebrew tradition this relation is compared to the relation of the ‚bone skeleton‘ (which is steady, enduring) to the ‚muscles and flesh‘ (moving). Here we have the ‚male and female‘ again, also seen as represented by all the so-called ‚positive and negative commandments‘, the ‚do's and don't's‘ of the Bible (numbered as 248 Do's or ‚bones‘ and 365 Don't's or ‚muscles‘, summing up to the 613 ‚commandments'/recommendations in total).

As in the common, ‚babylonian‘ Astrology, the standings of the planets inside the zodiacal signs, and the planets‘ mutual relations to each other, are the decisive factors of what one specific ‚horoscope‘ exhibits. But in comparison to the ‚babylonian‘ look on it, in the ‚Hebrew Astrology‘ the relations of planets to each other (especially ‚opposition‘, ‚conjunction‘ and ’square‘) are judged differently, almost contrarily.

An opposition is judged very good, because it is an opportunity for a ‚conversation‘ (out of which ‚fruit‘ can come) of the opposing planets/principles; but it remains only something very good, as long as the person doesn't know about it. And as soon as the person knows about it, it is said, it has ‚unfortunately become Snake‘ now, that means: the awareness has become the reason for an end of this conversing phase and leads over now to a new phase (referring to the biblical story of the beginning in the Garden, with the Serpent, the ‚Snake‘, that seduces Mankind ‚to fall‘ by promising them a certain knowledge).

A conjunction is judged as not so good (in contrary to the mutual enhancing effect of planets in conjunction, that is primarily seen in the babylonian method), because it has no dynamics. In such case it is recommended, to wait instead for the planets getting in some kind of opposition again.

A square means, that all planets in the four signs of the square are to be looked at as a ‚common potential‘; i. e. if one of the possibilities gets realized in a life situation, the others in that square always should be considered as being very likely to happen, too. So, a planet in a square constellation brings the other planets in that square with it, too, as potential opportunities, because of its ‚well-connectedness‘ with them through the square of the four zodiacal signs in which the square constellation happens to be.

With these three basic possibilities of constellation of the 7 planets you can already see many connections in the horoscope you are examining, if you know the deeper meanings of the planets and the zodiacal signs. In the following sections of this introduction we will look first at the three groups of the signs, after that at the 7 (visible) planets, and finally at the ‚hidden‘ planets, too, which are actually the most important factors for the Hebrew view on Astrology, because they can literally change EVERYTHING.

The First of the 3 Groups of the Zodiacal Signs: the 4 Female Signs

Now, after several basic concepts have been established in the first part, we slowly can start with going into the actual signs of the Zodiac. As already mentioned, contrary to the split-into-4 babylonian approach to the 12 zodiacal signs referring to the classical ‚four-elements-doctrine‘, from the Hebrew point of view these 12 spiritual qualities of the Zodiac are seen as grouped into THREE general divisions: 3 ‚male‘ signs, 4 ‚female‘ signs and 5 ‚fruit‘ or ‚child‘ signs, according to the numbers 3, 4 and 5, which in the Ancient Hebrew mindset are associated in their ‚absolute value‘ with these three concepts of a ‚thesis‘, an ‚antithesis‘, and then the ’synthesis‘ of them both.

These three groups though are described typically not in this exact order 3-4-5, but in the order of 4-3-5. This is the case, because from our human point of view, from out of this world of duality, out of this dark ’night side‘ of the cosmic day we are living in, we firstly are confronted with the physical world of nature all around us, with the concrete, appearing reality, which seems to be governed by causal laws and is coming from some point in the past, aiming for some point in the future, with this always changing so-called ’now‘, as our ‚present time‘, constantly fleeing from us. It is the world of development, where even the eternal principles of ‚Being‘ are living themselves out merely as an adventureous ‚Becoming‘. It is thus the ‚female‘ world, speaking in the symbolic language of the Ancients, which we are confronted with in the first place. Only with time and experience we see, that there is indeed another reality than this mere ‚horizontal‘ one of the measurable outer world: the ‚vertical‘ dimension, which we have inside us as the ‚hidden‘, the 'non-appearing‘ reality, which nevertheless is of undeniable influence on the outer world of appearance – at least the influence through our own physical actions, which are based on our respective inner reality, we cannot deny. In this moment we reach as an individual consciously the ‚male‘ side of the world, which is seemingly in constant contradiction, or at least in frequent conflict with the hard-physical ‚female‘ side of the outer world, the seemingly 'stronger‘ one.

And only, where these two worlds can unite within the individual's perception of life, the third dimension of reality is experienced: the ‚fruit‘, coming out of that, what seemed to be an opposition, but which now proved to be indeed a complementarity: a duality that needs both its extemes, with each of those extremes being in need of its complement ‚on the other side‘.

The 4 female, 3 male and 5 fruit signs are traditionally imagined as ordered in a ‚triangle‘, and by this the shape of their inner connections in the spiritual realm is expressed; which is a different connection than their connection as a ‚circle of star pictures on the sky‘ of the material realm (how the babylonian Astrology primarily looks at them). In so far, the triangle illustrating the ‚Pythagorean Theorem‘ is indeed the very ‚Triangle of Human Reality‘.

This ‚Triangle‘ could be summarized as follows: You are beginning 'naturally forced‘ by firstly following the horizontal line of the ‚female signs', and within those you go from the more transcendent, ‚mythical', to the more concrete, more immanent. Then while going this causally ‚forced', natural path of life, you begin (from an individually determined point on) consciously to ‚go upwards', too, up the vertical line of the ‚male signs'. In this dimension of experience you start from a first discovery of the heavenly origins of the earthly, then you are passing the insight into the present and future of Mankind (and of yourself), and by this you come finally more and more to an insight into the whole (spiritual) potential and destination of the earthly realm down here. And then – if both directions, horizontal and vertical, are perceived and realized as something ‚belonging together' all along – you ultimately enter the dimension of the ‚fruit signs', too. Here you now have to let converge the two other dimensions, the male and female, vertical and horizontal, on both their respective ‚other ends', too. With this ambition you are then going ‚back' on this 'new path', the ‚diagonal one', namely down on the ‚hypothenusis' of the fruit signs, and by this, merging together again the abstract and concrete, the vertical and the horizontal, the transcendent and immanent aspects of reality, to realize the fruit INSIDE this concrete world down here. So with this ‚impregnation' by the male principle ‚this world down here' becomes the ‚womb', in which ‚the fruit ripes', and from which this fruit finally is born as the ‚Child (of God)' into this world.

This look on reality is the reason for certain figures of speech in the ancient literature. For example, when a person never looks for the invisible side of the

30

world, but only takes for ‚real‘, what he/she can touch with his/her hands or at least measure with the ’scientific instruments‘ of his/her time … then this person (no matter whether that person is a male or a female) is called ‚a widow‘, because the person would be like ‚a woman, who has lost her husband‘, an appearing being, which has lost its ‚inner secret‘ (or the connection with it); and now she is only ‚a hollow appearance‘, without any deeper life inside. Contrarily, a person, who ONLY lives in the so-called ’spiritual realms‘, a fanatic mystic, fleeing and detesting the world … such a person would be called ‚a man, who never knew a woman in his life‘ (again, no matter whether that person is a male or a female); he is like ‚a mere idea‘, without realization. We could speak of the ‚widow‘ being essentially a ‚dead corpse‘, a body without any spirit inside enlivening it; and of the ‚unmarried man‘ as a ‚ghost‘, a mere spirit without a body expressing the spiritual in the appearance. From both of these pitiful examples no one can possibly expect any actual ‚fruit‘, as long as they remain ‚alone‘ in this sense.

The zodiacal signs are understood as a constant influence on the Earth, which herself is pictured exactly in the center of the circle of the 12 signs. But this influence in itself (without the planets moving through them, bringing the dynamics into this grand harmony) is only like a set of mere consonants of a language; it stays relatively ’silent‘, being only ’noises‘, no tone is there, or even a melody. It is the planets first, which, as the ‚vowels‘ of this language, are making the signs actually audible as sounds – and finally even as ‚words‘, carrying down to Earth actual meaning and sense.

31

Before we now finally begin with explaining (or rather ‚meditating on') the single zodiacal signs of the so-called ‚female' character, it will be useful to have another short detour from our main topic. Namely to have a look on the Hebrew alphabeth, on the 22 Hebrew letters as a system of numbers and word-pictures. Because several times we will have to refer to these Hebrew letters, when looking into the zodiacal signs and their meaning on the background of the hebrew and biblical worldview.

1. Aleph; 1 ‚(head of a) bull'

2. Beth; 2 ‚house; temple'

3. Gimel; 3 ‚camel; weaning; giving/granting'

4. Daleth; 4 ‚door; opening of a tent'

5. Heh; 5 ‚window; revelation'

6. Waw; 6 'nail; peg (of a tent)'

7. Zayin; 7 ‚weapon; arrow; paddle of a boat'

8. Cheth; 8 ‚to haul out, to tear out; fear, shocked'

9. Teth; 9 ‚womb; basket; potter's clay'

10. Yod; 10 ‚(acting) hand; arm'

11. Khaph; 20 ‚(receiving) hand(ful)'

12. Lamed; 30 ‚learning; teaching; oxen's staff (to control animals)'

13. Mem; 40 ‚water'

14. Nun; 50 ‚(a certain kind of) fish; sperm; seed'

15. Samekh; 60 ‚curled up (water-) snake'

16. Ayin; 70 ,eye; source/spring/well'

17. Phe; 80 ,mouth; command'

18. Tzade; 90 ,(fish)hook; just(ice)'

19. Quph; 100 ,monkey/ape; eye of a needle'

20. Resh; 200 ,(human) head; principle'

21. Shin; 300 ,tooth; flame of fire; to consume'

22. Thaw; 400 ,cross; sign; covenant'

Besides these basic values of the letters and the meanings of their names and symbols (originally mostly referring to the ancient picture symbols of the modern letters, too), there are a plenty of additional aspects to the letters, which here cannot be explained any further (like for instance the actual shape of the Hebrew character of the letter; or the sound of the letter, sometimes depending on its position in a word). Only it shall be said that. concerning additional number values, there are especially the ,Ath-Bash-values' of the letters (that means, the value of the A[leph],1, changed with that of the Th[aw], 400, that of the B[eth], 2, changed with that of the Sh[in], 300, and so on; so for the third letter Gimel this Ath-Bash-value would be the 200), the ,full values' of the letters (that is the letters of the fully spelled name of a letter counted together in their values; for example the Gimel is spelled G-M-L, so its ,full value' is $3+40+30=73$); and the ,great values' of the letters (for Gimel that would be Gimel Mem Lamed, so G-M-L and M-M and L-M-D, so $73+80+74 = 227$); and combinations of these values like the ,complete value' ('normal' value plus ,Ath-Bash' value; for Gimel that is 203). But most of these numbers and values are not important for the following introductory explanations of Hebrew Astrology anyways.

A last point to be mentioned here concerning the Hebrew Alphabeth and its letters is: Since the last sign of the 22 is the Thaw with the value 400 (so the principle of the 4, the Female, the concrete, worldly, earthly and appearing material dimension ,in the Hundreds'), there is the quite ,logical' expectation, that there might be a mystical '23rd sign' as representing the value 500 (that would be ,the 5, that is: the Fruit in the hundreds', also said to be the ,circumference of the Tree of Life' and the ,distance between Heaven and Earth'), which cannot be articulated or written in THIS world, because it transcends this world already in itself in every regard.

Now: The four ,Female Signs' of the Zodiac are basically of the character of the 'symbolic number 4', which is the number of the ,female principle' (see for example the ,4 elements', ,4 directions of the wind and 4 corners of the Earth', nowadays ,4 spacetime dimensions', etc.), the number of the ,female side of human reality': the ,horizontal' happenings in their timely development, ,cause-and-effect', all that is time-and-space-bound, concrete, material, visible, appearing, and by this ,revealing', too; it is the natural, the logical and the strictly causally ordered, governed by 'natural laws'.

While describing the signs, the focus will be on the more ,constructive' aspects of them. But of course there is always the possibility, too, to experience the influence of a sign in its destructive form. Typically this happens, when the true nature of the sign

34

influencing a situation or an individual is misunderstood. This danger of misunderstanding the potential of the spirit around us, will be mentioned only in one short paragraph in the end of the description of each sign. With the constructive aspects of every sign as the base, this respective danger of each will be easily understood, without putting this danger itself too much into focus.

The first female sign is Taurus. It is the ‚bull'; in Hebrew called 'shor' (which precisely means ‚a single bull', but sometimes used for both sexes of cows). Taurus is the 2nd sign of the zodiacal circle, how it is visible on the night sky and counted through the months of the year, beginning with the spring month of Aries (around March/April in the modern Roman sun calendar).

In this sign the world, how we (as 'self-conscious humanity', so to speak) perceive her, was created. But the world was not created in the BEGINNING of Taurus, but only around after the first third of the roughly 2150 years every age is lasting. That's why it is said: one part of this ‚heavenly bull' always ‚remains hidden outside this world'.

At this point it should be made clear with a few sentences that ‚time' and ‚ages' in the Bible are to be understood in a more general, ‚absolute', less concrete sense, than the time periods of our modern calendars. The word ‚year' (or ‚day') in the Bible refers not always to the exact same period of time, but the actual ‚lenght' of such a period is depending on the overall relation of the described happening to other happenings and developments in the biblical story, as well as it is depending on its relation to

35

ETERNAL principles. An example may make this more clear: never in the Bible there is a notion of something happening 'xyz years after the beginning of the world/after creation' (although it would be easy to calculate this by examining the detailed notions of the life ages of the descendants of Adam for example), in contrary there are only 'relative' notions of points and periods in time, like 'in the xyz^{th} year of the king Abc' or '480 years after the captivity in Egypt', etc. And to give a very simple example for the difference between 'relative' and 'absolute' periods of time: The (absolute) 'days' of the creation 'week' in the first chapter of Genesis, of course, cannot be defined in lenght by the sun and its appearence and its visible movement on the earthly sky (like we nowadays define that [relative] time period called 'one day'), since the sun, with the moon and the other stars, are only created on the 'fourth day' ... So the 'days' of creation week obviously mean an 'absolute' period of time, a principal 'stage', if you will.

This seemingly strange understanding of time in the Bible is necessary, because periods of time in the Bible are not (only) counted from their reality in THIS world (as 'historical' facts of developments), but from their 'absolute' reality, expressing an ETERNAL fact of existence, not only a circumstance happening somewhere inside a theoretically infinite line of time. That means, that the 5777 years since creation (till the year of 2017 a. D. of modern calendars) only are an exact number, 'if several discontinuities of time are taken into account', how it is explained.

36

One major characteristic of Taurus now is the ‚breaking through from somewhere hidden into the visible‘, just like our world is created somewhere within the age of Taurus, but is appearing already as something whole, in the middle of that age, like ‚out of the nothing‘ (or out of another level of reality). This aspect of Taurus is compared to the Aleph, the first Hebrew letter, which is not really pronouncable as long as it stands alone, but only when it comes along combined with a vowel (representing a planet). Taurus, as the beginning of anything, is a ’sudden birth‘ out of incomprehensible power, not describable in itself, only in relation to its accompanying effects.

That is, in a Taurus-oriented human being this ‚Taurus-layer‘ brings something into this world from out of ‚the other side‘, and namely brings this ’something‘ with a harsh, sometimes even with a brutal strenght of impact, which can make the fellow human beings feel insecure about it, as well as it can unsettle the Taurus-oriented human being itself by its inexplicable roughness of appearance.

Although a ‚female‘ sign, thus a sign of the more causal side of reality, in Taurus especially that part of causality appears, which is calculateable, predictable ONLY in statistical approaches, for the so-called ‚general cases‘ – but which is nonetheless very surprising and erratic in the concrete, special, unique situation. Here the ‚hidden part of the bull‘ is showing up as ‚the unexplainable‘ in a human beings life and in life in this world in general.

In this field of ‚erratic dangers‘ (and the fear of such) belong for instance all kinds of ‚accidents‘ in personal life, be it a fire in the basement, a lightning

37

striking the apple tree in the garden, or a sudden heart attack hitting a grandfather while playing football with his grandson. These kinds of accidents induced by Taurus are symbolically found in the Bible as ‚an ox that pushes‘; see therefore the precise ‚commandments’/recommendations (Exodus 21, 28ff), how to tread an ox that has hurt or killed a human, and what to do about the owner of such an ox, under which circumstances, and so on. Although we will never be able to prevent all such kind of accidents, we DO shall try to avoid at least as much as possible of them by keeping certain precautions (to give some profane examples: to have fire extinguishers at home, to turn off the water supply when leaving the house for longer periods, being careful what to eat as a diabetic, etc.). Although of course: the ‚coincidences‘ of life, that ‚hidden part of the bull‘, do not only appear as ‚badluck‘, but as ‚goodluck‘, too. And often both at the same time, if a situation is goodluck to one person, but badluck to another (for instance: because someone’s taxi cab is late at the airport, you get his seat instead of him, and maybe even as a low-priced ‚last minute‘ booking …).

Biblically, Taurus is described in more detail concerning its quality, by what happens in the first six chapters of the Bible (to be more precise: from Creation until the time, when Noah would be around 250 years old), especially in 4 great story lines: 1. Creation itself (Mankind as the perfect final point of the world’s manifestation); 2. the ‚Fall of Mankind‘ through a sudden and quick ‚loss of everything good, which Mankind had in the beginning‘ (because of the ‚Serpent‘ that introduces ’something new‘); 3. Cain

38

and Able (first/prototypical case of ‚murder‘; the more physical, bodily consciousness ‚killing‘ the spiritual consciousness in every human being very early in life); and 4. the so-called ‚Nephilim‘, the ‚Sons of God mixing with the Daughters of Mankind‘, breeding the ‚Fallen Ones‘ (also called: ‚Famous Ones‘, ‚Heroes‘ or ‚Strongmen‘; which can be described in essence as ‚potentially dangerous, very powerful forces inside this natural world, incorporated into actual beings‘, which are originally generated by the direct and ‚ungodly‘ influence of heavenly realities into this earthly realm; then being the main reason for the necessity of the ‚Great Cleansing‘ by means of the Flood).

The typical danger in the sign of Taurus is to be too scared of that ‚bull-power‘ inside oneself, or, projected onto the surrounding world: a fear of the basically uncontrollable nature of this whole material world and of our own life in here. But the solution to such fear can only be the acceptance of it: Yes, the raging bull IS dreadful, dangerous! But by this unpredictable force in the beginning ALL has been brought into existence, so trust, that that bull has his purpose for you, too. So maybe grab the ‚red rag‘ and dare that ‚bull fight‘ as the ‚Torero‘! On the other hand: sometimes not daring the fight, even avoiding it, can be the better choice, too. And by this you instead would be connecting to the ‚defencelessness‘ of the next sign, the ‚Lamb‘ Aries; the ‚defencelessness‘ as one (often underestimated) potential path to salvation.

The second female sign then, Aries, is the very first sign of the year in the visible zodiacal circle. In

Hebrew the sign Aries, the ‚ram‘, is called rather ‚taleh‘ (which means ‚male lamb‘), so here the youth, the meekness is in the focus of the name, not so much the ‚grown up mighty ram with its impressive horns‘.

The ‚Lamb‘ as this very first sign of the Zodiac is perceived as ‚the true foundation of the world‘. You can discover this view of the Lamb as the ‚Foundation of All‘ in the wording ‚Lamb of God‘ as a reference to the Messiah, Jesus in the New Testament, who is seen as being 'slaugthered from before the beginning of the world‘ to guarantee salvation out of that world (Revelation 13, 8) and as the one and only ‚Foundation Stone‘ (Isaiah 28, 16; 1 Corinthians 3, 11; 1 Peter 2, 4-8).

It is especially the famous 'silence of the lamb‘ (specifically facing his slaughterer, too), which is stressed in the Hebrew tradition concerning this zodiacal sign. So it comes, that the ‚Lamb‘ is actually the very first sign, but so 'silent‘, that it can only appear as the second, after Taurus brought the world into being already by its outer-worldly sudden force. With a look on the Hebrew alphabeth it is then said: the sign of the lamb is already ‚before‘ the first letter of the Hebrew alphabeth (which is the Aleph, the ‚[head of a] bull‘), because the 22 letters only describe the ‚female‘, the concrete world of appearance. But the ‚Lamb‘ as the Foundation of All is actually of something more primordial, not of this appearing world, as already the bull is only partly from this world, only perceiveable in combination with ‚the vowels‘, not in itself. The mystical Lamb is even more ‚unspeakable‘ than that.

40

This Lamb of the Zodiac is like the primeval Unity of the human being and of whole Mankind with the Source: coming into our world of time and space in this sign, bringing with it this unity as something not logically graspable, but still somehow perceiveable, feelable, as a deep ‚longing for the origin', for the Source we flow from. By this, the Lamb is a symbol for the Redemption of the individual.

For the further elaboration of this aspect of the zodiacal Lamb as the Redeemer we can read the story of Abraham and Isaac in the Bible (Genesis 22): here the mystery is expressed as ‚the ram in place of the son'. Because in this story of the ‚Binding of Isaac', it is the ‚ram, which is caught by the horns in the bush' (Genesis 22, 13), which replaces the son as the actual offering, and which then instead of the son disappears into another ‚world' or ‚level of existence' – as soon as Abraham actually was WILLING to even sacrifice his ‚own son' (= his own future in this world of matter). By the way: the actual term in the Bible for the so-called ‚human sacrifice' of Isaac is NOT ‚burnt offering', but literally a ‚rising upwards'. And the symbol of the ‚binding of Isaac' is, that it is a ‚binding the four extremities together', as a ‚collecting the 4 into the 1' (1-4-principle, see first part of this introduction); and then a readiness for ‚cutting the head off', that is ‚ending the circulation of the blood through the body', as the ambition for ‚breaking the cycle' of this infinite time world (‚of the 4').

Speaking about the Lamb in the Bible, it is eye-catching that the lamb occurs as the most common sacrifice animal. In the Hebrew tradition an ‚animal'

41

always refers to the human body, respectively to certain parts of it. So an ‚animal sacrifice' means in the spiritual sense, to bring the own bodily existence into a service of the Eternal, not to remain only in ‚mental gymnastics' and ‚theological philosophizing', but to actually draw consequences of your belief, reaching deep into your everyday life, that is: into what you daily do with your body, your physical side of existence as a human. The Hebrew word for sacrifice, ‚qurban', means actually ‚(something) to approach, to come near', implying the conscious approach of the human being towards his Creator, his Source.

And one of the most famous and certainly most important sacrifices of the biblical storyline is the so-called ‚Passah-Lamb' (Exodus chapter 12): a ‚Lamb in every house' as necessity for the redemption of the People of God out of ‚Egypt', out of the enslavement by the world of duality. And this redemption is happening expressively NOT out of own power, but it is a surprising, even unexpectable Godly Salvation. It is the ‚moaning and lamenting' of the Children of Israel, that ‚moves the Eternal's heart' to make this happen. And it is only possible, where the ‚Lamb' is ‚inside the house'; and the Hebrew word for ‚house' is the ‚Bejth', written just like the second letter ‚Beth' in the Alphabeth, the ‚B' with the numeric value of 2. So the ‚Lamb' must be present WITHIN (the world of) ‚Duality', otherwise the ‚Destroyer' will strike the ‚inhabitants of that house' (see Exodus 12, 23).

The Lamb thus expresses in his 'silence before the butcher' a ‚redemption through devotion', the

42

‚victory of defencelessness'. That means, that in this sign the essential breakthrough is reached not by force, not by power, not by own effort and struggle – but by the ‚letting go' of oneself, by the unshakeable meekness of a ‚rather being slaughtered than being rebellious (against destiny/God)'-mentality.

And then this Lamb brings a delightful surprise: that after the commitment to the (self-)sacrifice, it becomes clear, that your (and be it ‚only' figuratively spoken) ‚being slaughtered', this ‚rising upwards', does not mean to actually ‚leave this world' as a whole, but to gain a full new form of life down here on Earth, only freed now from the never-ending cycle of toil and from the searching for meaning and happiness in purely physical states of being. It is a 'silent peace', which maybe never will be understood, or even believed by the surrounding world to be there at all. But it is there.

That's why it is said concerning the Lamb: ‚When you think you are going to die, the Lamb appears' – and by this experience you realize the presence of an ‚either AND or'-reality, instead of the 'normally expected' mere ‚either-or-opposition': in the heavenly realm, in the Eternal, there is BOTH together, the ‚disappearing' here, ‚rising upwards' out of this world of time, but nevertheless 'staying present here' (also compare this experience with the Hebrew word for ‚Heaven', which was already explained in the first part of this introduction, concerning one of its translations as ‚fire AND water' in a ‚contra-intuitive', non-earthly kind of harmony).

The typical danger in this sign of the Zodiac is to look at the Lamb in his adult state as ‚the mighty ram

43

with its horns'. Then a Lamb could feel to be obliged to ‚fight the struggle' with own power, instead of being devote to his destiny, in meekness. The Lamb then would be confusing himself with Capricorn, a sign, which indeed sometimes has to fight in its own power. But the ram/lamb should NOT fight, but should be mild and even surrender … to win in the end just by this courage to take even the risk of being slaughtered. The re-connecting with the Taurus-layer in oneself can help here, too: to understand, that there is another part in yourself, that indeed HAS the great power out of ‚the other side'; but what NOW is needed, as the Lamb (although brought here from that ‚other side', too), is rather the original united-ness with the Source, than that primordial power of Taurus. Both signs have their respective purpose, being the two sides of ONE primeval unity, which had to split to be able to appear in this world of duality.

Now the third female sign is Pisces, which is on the 12th position in the zodiacal circle. Its name means fish (in the plural), in Hebrew ‚dagim' (which also means ‚fish' in the plural); and typically it is pictured as two fish swimming in opposite directions, more or less mirroring each other.

To approach the deeper meaning of this sign from the Hebrew perspective, it should be firstly established that ‚water' always is associated with ‚time'. For example the Hebrew letter ‚Mem', with the numeric value of 40, can also be pronounced and written as ‚mayim', which actually means ‚water' in Hebrew. And the number 40 (as well as the 400) is very often used in the Bible to describe a ‚large (or even

44

infinite) amount of time' (see for example the '40 years of wandering through the wilderness', the '40 days of disappearance of Moses', when he is alone on the mountain with God; and in the New Testament the '40 days of fasting in the wilderness' of the Messiah right after his baptism). This 40-symbolism refers back to the principle of the ‚4 as the highest number in this world of Duality', as explained in the first part of this introduction.

So, that ‚time', which is meant here with ‚water' and with the number 40, is always understood with the focus on the strictly ‚linear character' of it, so it is generally the time which is bound on our understanding of 3D-space, the ‚unfree' understanding of a flowing time, which ‚takes everything it reaches', ‚banning it' into the so-called ‚past', never ‚giving it back to the present' – and with time itself the ‚water'-symbol can mean the whole WORLD of time with its limiting and structuring laws of nature and society.

Pisces is the most ‚physical', immanent sign of the 4 female ones. While Taurus and Aries are somehow ‚transcendent' still, more representing certain aspects from the ‚other side', which in these signs are present for THIS world, too (and then Aquarius later is already leaving this purely material world of time and space again), the Pisces-quality lies especially in the very earthly acceptance of matter, time and space as such – ‚the fish feels good' in his element, the water, the time. But this acceptance of time and space and feeling at home here does not mean, that Pisces is fulfilled in this world alone. In contrary, it is especially the fish out of all beings in the waters,

45

which has a high possibility to get ‚fished out of the water‘, because the ‚fishermen‘ know, that the fish ‚bears the secret‘; the secret, which only can be revealed after being fished out (a famous tale about King Solomon will be told in the following part of this introduction, wherein the theme of ‚a fish bearing the secret‘ is very essential).

With regard to this possibility of ‚a fish being fished out of the waters‘ it is said, that the fish itself is only half of the sign of Pisces, the other half is indeed the fisherman, who strives to fish the fish out of the water, ‚out of time‘ into the ‚realm of eternity‘, where its ‚inner secret‘ can be revealed.

And practically this ‚fishing-out‘ is accomplished with a certain ‚tool‘, namely with a ‚hook‘. And the Hebrew word for ‚hook‘ is the name of the 18th letter of the Alphabeth, ‚Tzade‘, which is closely related to the word for a ‚Wise One‘ (or more precisely ‚Righteous One‘, or ‚Proven One‘), who is called a ‚Tzadiq‘. A truely ‚Wise One‘ in the Hebrew understanding is therefore someone who ‚fishes you out of the waters‘, brings you to an experience of eternity. And this means, a Wise One can only exist as such ‚on the other side‘, ‚in the inner world‘, because the fisherman can not fish the fish, when he himself is under the water. So no actual human being as a person appearing in this outside world of time and space (… that is: ‚a world of water‘) will be a ‚Wise One‘ him-/herself, but at best, ‚the Wise One inside him or her‘ can help you to find contact to ‚the Wise One inside yourself‘.

On this background it is easily comprehensible, why in the New Testament there are so many examples for the ‚fish and fishing‘.symbolism. Important passages, where Jesus himself refers (with words or deeds) to ‚fish‘ and ‚fishing‘ are for instance: the ‚fish with a coin inside‘ (the ‚hidden secret, only revealed, when on the land‘; see Matthew 17, 27); fishermen as His first disciples, ‚becoming fishers of men‘ (Matthew 4, 19: ‚Follow me, and I will make you fishers of men!‘); catching much fish with a great ’net, cast into the sea‘, then ‚taking the good ones and throwing the bad ones away‘, as a parable for the ‚Kingdom of God‘ (the ’net‘) and how it is in effect in ‚this world of time‘ (the ’sea of water‘), rescueing human souls (the ‚fish‘) out of it (Matthew 13, 47-50).

The longing of the fish for ‚being fished out‘ is expressing itself for a human being in this sign of the Zodiac as a tendency to ‚mysticism‘, a desire for ‚the other side‘ of existence. In the right way understood, this ‚being fished out of time‘ though does not mean, to be brought ‚from time-experience to an experience of eternity‘ as a singular event, but the true Mystic would strive to ‚be fished out of the water over and over again‘. He wants to know all the other ‚waters‘, too, and always again wants to be fished out of those, too, as an everlasting journey through all the waters and all the dry lands!

He does not believe anymore that the surface of his sea, which he only sees from down here under the water, is the actual ‚Heaven‘ (although he indeed may get a slight impression of the actual sky above the sea already through this surface of the water); he knows: … the TRUE heaven is a whole new world out of the waters of his sea; but in this outside world, his own sea, too, is an essential part of the landscape!

And beside this there are many other waters, rivers, lakes and oceans, even clouds in the skies with amounts of water pouring down every now and then, nourishing the dry areas of this world outside the waters ... So in ,Heaven' there is ,water' (= time), too. Not a conincidence that the Hebrew word for Heaven, ,Sh'mayim' (which we already understood as being a combination of ,fire and water'), can be translated as ,there is water', too (then pronounced 'sham mayim', but spelled still exactly the same).

The typical danger of Pisces is that the human being under its influence feels so comfortable in this ,world of water', that he/she does not want to be fished out of the water at all, and may even ,be hiding in the depths' of time(-and-space-world and -life(style)), to avoid being fished out by the ,Zadiq'. This hiding fish however will be experiencing an inner (maybe unconscious) conflict, because actually the fish WANTS to be found, to be fished out, it is part of the fish's inner destination (and that means on the personal level: one wants to be known and appreciated as a SPIRITUAL being, too, not only as a purely ,physical appearance' and a mere 'social existence' out of many).

In such a case this ,fish' maybe must experience for the first time, how ,the light of the sun shines through the surface of his sea deep into the waters', enlightening this world of time a little bit more and by this, directing the attention of the fish ,to the surface of the water', and to what may be beyond that surface, granting such a beautiful light! And maybe the next ,fisherman's hook', sinking down from up there into this fish's water world, will be tempting

48

enough – due to ‚that cord on it', seemingly leading upwards towards ‚the shining disc of light' beyond the surface …

The fourth (and final) female sign is Aquarius, the so-called ‚water carrier'. In Hebrew this sign is called ‚dli', which means just ‚bucket' (that is the bucket, by which the ‚water carrier' scoops, carries and then pours out the water). It is the 11th of the signs of the zodiacal circle on the sky.

By the ‚Bucket' the ‚water' (which we know by now as being a symbol for the ‚time') gets controllable, manageable to a certain degree. That means, in this sign – although still in this world of time, space and matter – the human being is getting more and more ‚free' from the force and pressure of this worldly bounds. The time is still present of course, but it plays not the active part any more, it gets ‚passive', is being handled by the ‚Bucket'. And the symbol of the ‚Man pouring out the waters' does not mean, that this is a singular act and then ‚there is no more time' … no, this ‚pouring out' happens again and again, the ‚Man' (representing every human beings INNER existence) indeed feels joy in handling time in this active way.

In Judaism there is a tradition to celebrate the last of the biblical Feasts (‚Sukkoth', also known as the ‚Feast of the Tabernacles') with a ceremony, whereby water gets scooped out of a source and poured out again in great joy (see also Isaiah 12, 3). This last Feast of the yearly cycle represents (in one of its meanings) the final ‚coming together' of Heaven and Earth as the ‚Holy Wedding' in the end of times, when the difference, the opposition between Heaven

49

and Earth, between Eternity and Time, is finally revealed to be illusionary, that in Heaven BOTH is present in harmony together, not as a contradiction.

By the way: one of the Hebrew words for 'salvation, rescue' is ‚dlia‘, derived from the word for ‚bucket‘, so ‚rescueing‘ someone is understood as ‚bucketing‘, scooping someone out of the waters …

‚Freedom from time and space‘ means not, that there are no more time and space at all. Only, time and space are not taken too seriously anymore, they are accepted as limiting and structuring principles, which have a senseful purpose. Not as a ‚cage‘, but as the walls of a house you live in: you know, you can leave it, if you want, but inside you have your security from certain ‚dangers‘, or rather ‚challenges‘, of the outside. And it would be stupid to tear down the walls, only to ‚feel more free‘ … therefore you have all the doors and windows of the house; you only have to remember them and use them, when you feel this desire for the outside world, without wanting to leave your house for good yet. Like ‚time‘ separating the happenings in this world from each other, 'space' in this world may be separating the beings from each other – but at the same time it is CONNECTING everything in its common realm, making it possible to ‚meet each other‘.

Freedom from time and space means indirectly also ‚freedom from the law (of nature), and, in a more biblical, spiritual sense, ‚freedom from the commandments of the Bible, of the Thorah‘, too (from this perspective the Letter to the Romans by the Apostle Paul in the New Testament can be understood in its true depths; see Romans chapters

7+8). And again, not in the sense, that there is NO MORE law, but in the sense, that living according to the ‚law‘ (= to the recommendations) sets you free from the limitations which would come upon you, where you go against the law and in consequence suffer the necessary corrections of your behaviour through an outer force, enpowered by the law you broke. So it is actually this ‚outer force‘ of the law, what you get liberated from in the sign of the water carrier, of the ‚bucket‘: the water, the TIME, in which the consequences of the law and its trespassing are experienced, becomes ‚manageable‘ by means of that bucket. Instead of an ‚outer force‘, it becomes an inner, volontary force inside you, that corrects you deliberately – and by this you gain an ability to ‚make some exceptions to the law‘ for yourself, where it serves the deeper meaning of the whole. These exceptions you cannot force upon anyone else, but for your own behaviour you can always choose to follow them, as long as they are in harmony with your own inner experience of ‚the law‘.

Especially the ‚inner time‘ is then no longer bound so closely to the outwardly. That means, experiencing joy for instance can endure easily inside yourself even in times, when ‚outside‘ there is no more reason for joy. And this outer situation is looked at now as something merely 'structuring‘, too, like the walls of your house are: they are structuring the potential of your individual destiny, which you live out within this framework according to your own will – it is only the ‚raw material‘ to be formed by yourself.

Like the size and type of the canvas and the colours and the kind of the paint is structuring the potential

51

for a new painting by a ‚poor‘ painter, who can't efford his own stuff and so just ‚takes what he gets‘ from friends and by-walkers, donating him the material for his art. But maybe … he even decides himself to be that ‚poor‘, because especially out of this seemingly ‚coincidental‘ factor to his art, he gains his creativity?!

The typical danger of this sign is, not accepting itself as one of the ‚female‘, earthly signs. A human being heavily influenced by Aquarius sometimes wants to be only ‚transcendent‘ and spiritual, not accepting, that there will always be ‚more water‘ to fill in the bucket and pour it out again, that he/she will never ‚have poured out ALL of the water‘, never will get completely away from time and space and the natural laws, as long as he/she lives in this physical body. If this human being tries to flee this reality, there is a tendency to ‚lose earth contact‘ more and more – and from some point on this would mean, to become indeed ‚insane‘ in the perception of this world. The solution here is only, to connect with the ‚Pisces-layer‘ in yourself: learn from the fish the joy of swimming through the waters, as well as being fished out of them! Then you will find the joy in the endless filling and emptying your bucket, too …

As a final topic for this chapter concerning the four female signs, it shall be looked at the general epochs of ‚our‘ history here in time and space, and how they fit in the scheme of the four female signs.

As already said, the creation of this world (of time and space, as we collectively perceive and experience it as 'self-conscious Mankind‘) happens in the middle of Taurus as something 'sudden‘, directly bringing into being highly developed cultures like Ancient Egypt, and similar on the other continents, too (see for example the many pyramidal buildings all over the Earth).

Aries, the ‚Lamb‘; then essentially represents the epoch of the most part of the so-called ‚Old Testament‘ of the Bible, or to be more exact: from around the ‚Great Flood‘ until (almost) ‚Jesus‘: a time of ‚angels visiting humans and other miracles‘ …

And then there is a ‚great shift‘ during this ‚transition‘ from the more ‚mythological, transcendent‘ signs Taurus and Aries to the rather ‚historical, immanent‘ signs Pisces and Aquarius, the shift that is also implied by the odd jump ‚from the 2nd and 1st to the 12th and 11th sign‘ of the cycle of the Zodiac. This shift happens to be not exactly, but at least approximately around the ‚year zero‘ of our modern calendars; probably around one or two centuries earlier, it is nothing exact to calculate. So we can call this the 'shift from mythological time to historical time of Mankind‘.

The ‚tearing apart of the curtain before the Holy of Holies in the Temple of Jerusalem‘, which is reported to have happened at the moment of Jesus‘ death on the cross, can be understood as ‚the materially manifest symbol‘ of that great transition from the 2 first to the 2 last signs of the Zodiac in human history (see Matthew 27, 51; Marc 15, 38; Luke 23, 45). And by the way: It is remarkable that, since Jesus, the use of language, the wording of the Bible, is turning much more ‚personal‘, now speaking directly to the individual, not anymore only ‚mythologically‘ to the whole ‚People of God' as a group, that is, to Mankind as a whole, like in the so-called ‚Old Testament'.

The Pisces-era then is the historical development of the last biblically described times of humanity until (almost) now; so it is the time of human history, where we actually have more or less solid facts about the happenings (that means: not having to deal with all too much ‚myths' and ‚legends', which are mixed into the ‚historical records', like in the ancient Egyptian ‚kings' lists' or in records like the ‚Tibetan Book of Death' or the ‚Mahabharata' …).

Aquarius now is OUR sign of the epoch since a few decades, in which time and space indeed become more and more ‚irrelevant' to a certain degree, ‚manageable' easily (first by means of technologies like the telegraph, the telephone, later television and now even internet, first only stationary, today even as 'smart phones' and other transportable devices; including things like photographies and videos, too, as possibility to ‚catch' moments in time out of the stream of time, making them available throughout space; … and not to forget airplanes, making journeys a matter of a few hours, which 100 years ago were a matter of weeks or months; etc.).

We can see now: The four Female Signs of the Zodiac are representing ‚the Whole World' (of time, space and matter; this ‚world of duality') in her development through time; from being established for us here ‚out of the nothing' (Taurus, the ‚Bull'), bringing with it something of the Eternal Source and a feeling of Oneness with this Source (Aries, the ‚Lamb'); but this only follows after the initial

54

‚breakthrough', as the unfolding of an unspeakable ‚Before' being remembered, the ‚living out of a giant myth' by early Mankind, so to speak … Then there is a drastic shift and that myth comes to an end, ‚history' as we know it comes into play; instead of ‚Angels and Devils', stories are told now about ‚Roman Emperors and Barbarian Rebels', Mankind seems to be feeling very ‚at home' in this world of linear time and its more and more explainable laws (Pisces, the ‚Fish') … but nowadays these finally ‚accepted' time and space become even slowly ‚circumstantial' again, to a certain degree at least, Mankind gets more and more in control of ‚the waters' (Aquarius, the ‚Bucket')…

And maybe we see the four Female Signs as well as representing the individuals stages of life, from natural birth till natural death, from childhood through adolescence and adulthood into a (hopefully) wise age towards the end of one's years: As a child ‚feeling thrown into this world', out of the primordial power of physical generativity, thereby bringing many unexplaineable abilities, as well as weaknesses with oneself (Taurus), growing into a unique character in the years of youth, as close to one's ideals, longings and hopes, as never again in later times of life (Aries), then at some point 'suddenly' being confronted with the 'seriousness' of adult life, with ‚paying bills' and 'social expectations', and during that: looking for the ‚meaning of all that' in a place beyond this everyday-waves of monotony (Pisces) … and finally (hopefully) reaching a state of consciousness, where all the boundaries and limitations of life and this world are not only accepted, but even appreciated as the necessary background structure, within which by now a whole great life of many adventures and miracles has already been possible to happen – and by telling the story of your own life (and be it only to yourself) you are ‚writing your story even anew‘ to some degree, ‚changing‘ your past by explaining it deliberately in a new and broader sense (Aquarius), knowing the outcome of it by now, seeing ‚the hand of God in your life‘, when looking actively backwards …

But these 4 stages of the female signs of course are only describing the experience of the individual on the linear, the ‚horizontal‘ level, and they are never EXACTLY distinguishable from each other, have rather flowing transitions into each other and even are going parallel sometimes. Beside this, as only ‚horizontal‘ descriptions, they are in reality always incomplete as a description of an actual persons life. Because there necessarily is the ‚vertical‘ side of experience, too, for every single human being. And this vertical experience is expressed in the ‚Male‘ Signs of the Zodiac, which shall be presented in the following part.

The Second of the 3 Groups of the Zodiacal Signs: the 3 Male Signs

The three ‚male' signs of the Zodiac, in the Hebrew approach to it, are Virgo, Libra and Scorpio. The number 3 is, as already established, perceived as the number of the ‚male (= inwardly, hidden, spiritual) principle'. And this triad is especially associated with the so-called ‚6th, 7th and 8th day of creation week', as presented in the very first part of this introduction.

So these male signs are very strongly bound to each other, as a unity of the three, which is obviously contrary to the harsh split in the row of the four signs of the female character, where there is that sharp shift particularly between the reality of Taurus and Aries as the first half (consisting of the 2nd and the 1st sign of the circle) and the reality of Pisces and Aquarius as the second half (consisting of the 12th and the 11th sign of the circle).

The strict unity of the three male signs is explained by the biblical recommendation (‚law') of the so-called 'sabbathical year', or more correctly 'shmittah year' (see Exodus 23, 10-11; Leviticus 25, 1-7; on the superficial interpretation this law is especially concerning the ‚agricultural life' of the Israelites after reaching the Promised Land), which recommends to ‚let the land rest in the seventh year', that is, to not sow nor reap in every seventh year.

This goes with the promise, that the harvest from the sixth year will be so rich, that it will last until there is new harvest again. That means, it will last for the sixth year itself, for the seventh year, in which nothing shall be harvested nor sowed, AND for the

57

eigth year, when it will be sowed again, but not yet harvested, because there was nothing sowed in the past year.

We already established the basic characteristics of the 6th, the 7th and the coming 8th ‚day of creation‘ in the first part of this introduction. Exactly these three ‚days‘ now are associated with the 6th, 7th and 8th sign of the natural circle of the Zodiac, Virgo, Libra and Scorpio, the three ‚male signs‘ in the Hebrew understanding of the Zodiac. We also looked very shortly on the whole complex of the 'seven days‘, of the complete ‚week of creation‘ in the very beginning of the Bible (Genesis 1,1-2,3), and at the fact it has a certain schematic structure of ‚2 times 3‘ days plus the 1 day of ‚rest‘, which represents ‚our world of time and space‘.

Now we will try to deepen this understanding of the ‚creation week‘ and its relevance for our human perception of reality. For this purpose we look at the system of the so called ‚Sephiroth‘, a word, which is translateable roughly as ‚cyphers, numerals‘ or as 'spheres‘, and which refers to the several levels of our reality, which all work together to form in their totality what we call our ‚7th day‘, the ‚world‘ in our human perception.

These Sephiroth (we will focus on the 7 out of them, which correspond to the 7 days of creation week and to the seven planets) are nothing which could be described on a completely rational, logical way, but the understanding of them is something which has to be built up rather by means of stories, comparisons and allegories. So it is nothing graspable solely by

58

the intellect, but only by a combination of intellect and a more ‚associative' understanding, like the kind of understanding needed to approach the symbols and happenings of a dream, a myth or a tale.

When we have established a solid foundation of these ‚Sephiroth', and by this a deeper insight into the importance of our ‚7th day', it will be much easier to handle the three ‚male' signs of the Zodiac, which are essentially representing the possibility of individually overcoming the ‚world of the seven days' in human life, and by this reaching the coming ‚world of the 8th day' (which is equated with the ‚experience of the Messiah', the bringer of 'salvation'). And this foundation will be a great help later, too, when we are looking at the seven visible planets in the fifth part of this introduction.

To get a basic overview, we start with a list of the 7 Sephiroth of the creation week's days and of their respective corresponding concepts (that is: the Hebrew names of the concepts, and one or two possible english translations). There are different possible counting modes of the Sephiroth: They can be counted as 10 (which is the most common number given), as 11 (with a ‚hidden' Sephiroth of ‚mystical knowledge' included) or as only 7, which we will now focus on. In this last mode of counting, the upper 3 or 4 Sephiroth (which are called ‚kether', ‚chokhmah', ‚binah' and the mystical ‚da'ath') are excluded as ‚transcendent', as ‚before visible creation'. But still especially the very first of these upper ones, ‚kether' (meaning ‚crown'), is appearing in the scheme of the lower 7, too, because the 7th Sefirah, the lowest of all, reconnects in the very end with the most high again, as fulfilling the purpose of creation, as ‚reaching the 8th day‘, the ‚unity of the origin‘, but now after the whole experience of being divided into the manifoldness throughout the world of the seven days.

The scheme of the seven Sephiroth is composed of two triangles, one above the other, both with the tip downwards, and then the seventh Sefirah alone under the lower triangle's tip:

2–1

–3–

5–4

–6–

–7–

Now, the names of the Sephiroth are:

In the first row, on the right side, ‚day 1‘: chesed (kindness, love)

First row, on the left side, ‚day 2‘: geburah (justice; strength)

In the second row, in the middle under the first two Sephiroth, ‚day 3‘: tiphereth (beauty; shine)

In the third row, on the right side, ‚day 4‘: netzach (victory)

Third row, on the left side, ‚day 5‘: hod (shape; praise)

Fourth row, in the middle under the 4th and 5th Sephiroth, ‚day 6‘: jesod (foundation)

And at the lowest point of the scheme, under the 6. Sephirah, ‚day 7‘: malkhuth (kingdom)

… and, as already mentioned, this last Sephirah of ‚malkhuth‘ is potentially called ‚kether malkhuth‘, too; then it is the 8th day, the reconnection to the ‚crown‘ of the transcendent, ‚upper Sephiroth‘.

Now it is said: All 7 Sephiroth are present together in the 7th Sefirah of our world of time and space, but in this 7th sphere everything is unconscious. Our consciousness as human beings is located in the 6th Sefirah, where we are ‚created‘ as human beings (on the 6th day of creation week), and where we eat of the ‚tree of knowledge of good and evil‘, by which our ‚eyes are opened‘ (see Genesis 3,7).

All these 7 spheres, or ‚levels of existence‘, run parallel in the human being. During the ’normal‘ perception of everyday life, we cannot separate the respective experiences of the different spheres from each other. But by taking some distance to look at them, we can get a basic insight.

For this purpose, to approach the characteristics of each of these spheres, it will take a wide spectrum of perspectives on each of these Sephiroth. For the beginning now, we will look at one little story of the Ancients, which is illustrating the circular character of our reality and the importance of every step of the cycle for the experience as a whole; and then we will take one slightly deeper look at the seven biblical figures representing the 7 sephiroth and their respective qualities.

That old story goes like this:

My father bought me a little lamb for the price of two Sus.

Then the cat came and bit the lamb dead.

The dog saw it, and bit the cat.

The stick saw it, and beat the dog.

The fire saw it, and burned the stick.

The water saw it, and extinguished the fire.

The ox saw it, and drank away the water.

The man sees all that, and he slaughters the ox.

Now, THAT is seen by the Angel of Death, and he takes away the man out of this life.

God sees the Angel doing that – and takes away the Angel of Death.

So far the story. We see: There is the ‚Lamb of the foundation‘ we already spoke about in the last part of this introduction. It is bought for a price of ‚Two‘, because in the beginning there always has to be the ’split‘, the duality. And the lamb has to die, for the ‚journey‘ to begin. And in the end of the journey, ‚death‘ himself is taken away – but only AFTER ‚Man(kind) died‘. Between these two points of ‚the lamb being slaughtered before the beginning‘ and ‚death being taken away by God, through the dying of Man‘ the whole world of the seven days takes place, the ‚7 Sephiroth‘ are enfolding.

We now want to look at these seven spheres and days from a second, a closer perspective, aiming for an understanding of the respective ‚complex of experiences‘ in more detail, which is present in each of those seven stages:

1: chesed; Abraham (Genesis 11,27-25,10); the mythical planet Sun; ,the cat which bites the lamb dead', the unavoidable and inexplicable ,magical' start of All (corresponding to the 'serpent in the Garden, making Mankind fall', too).

This first ,complex of experiences' is the unexpected breakthrough, a beginning out of nothing, or out of a 'supernatural loving kindness', out of grace and the pure will to give.

Abraham is said to find the connection to God without a teacher, without mediation or guidance or instruction; just out of himself. An old saying goes: The true Abraham you will only find when you are 50 years old. That means, that you won't find ,chesed', this loving kindness without a cause, in this world of the 7 alone, not even in the ,fulfilled 7' (which is the '49', see first part of this introduction), but only, when you are breaking through to the ,8th,, to the number (= the quality) AFTER the fulfilled 7, the $7 \times 7 + 1$, the '50'.

This sphere of Abraham not only contains ,Abraham himself', but ALL the experience and all the contacts, Abraham has in his story. He especially is the one, who has the great promises: to inherit the promised land, to have a son from his (seemingly ,too old') wife Sarah; but then he has to stay a foreigner in that promised land until his own death, and he has to bring his beloved son up the mountain where he is going to sacrifice him. He surely is desperate throughout much of his lifetime, believing in all the great promises, but so often being disappointed, not

63

understanding, what God wants with all that. But since he never TRIES to understand everything, he nevertheless always stays a perfect example for true faith, testifying for his unshakeable trust in the God of Heaven and Earth. This trust, without any evidence, is what characterizes the Sephirah of Abraham, ,chesed'. But the dangers of this Sephirah are not to be overlooked; these dangers are found in the parts of Abrahams story, where he himself doubts, or where other people want to harm him, and so on. These ,other people' of course are inside every one of us, too, just like ,Abraham' is. For all the following Sephiroth this basic assumption equally has to be taken into account: inside yourself there are always present ,the shadows', the enemies of the respective Sephirah's ,title figure', too …

2: geburah; Isaac (Genesis 21,1-35,29); the mythical planet Moon; ,the dog punishing the obviously evil cat', the logical consequence, the rational side of nature and Mankind, the ,law' governing measureable reality.

The beginning of chesed ,out of pure, giving love' gets its sustainability by the second Sephirah, by ,geburah', which is ,justice; strenght', the strenght of a law that sustains order and justice. This sphere is examplified by the biblical account of Isaac, Abrahams beloved son, who comes, as the result of Abrahams graceful devotion based on nothing ,rational', as the more rational factor that finally brings fulfillment, or rather confirmation of the hope.

In the tradition it is said: from the side of Isaac you meet the person, who will be a good teacher for you, who will accomplish to convince you, that ,it is all

64

good with THIS world, too, nonetheless'.

One obvious danger of this sphere is, to become too passive in your doing, like Isaac is rather passive in all his experiences, in the end even leading to the blessing of the ,wrong son' (from his human perspective).

3: tiphereth; Jacob/Esau (Genesis 25,21-50,13); the mythical planet Mars; ,the wooden stick, trying to force the dog under its will', the tools of Mankind's creativity used either as weapons for suppression, or as ordering principles taming the ,wild animalistic', as well as the ,heartless logical' inside ourselves.

The fruit of Isaac, the result of the 'strenght of justice', then is something ambivalent: Jacob AND Esau, the twins, who already in the mother's womb start fighting each other (see Genesis 25,22). Esau is that part in every human being, which strives for a prey, for a booty all the time, the ,hunter' on the search for the (4-legged) animals. He is never coming to rest, because this ,4-ness' of our world cannot be caught for ever, there will always be ,the next animal' to hunt. The brother of Esau is Jacob; he is the ,mild one', rather 'staying in the tent' (see Genesis 25,27). He represents the more subtle force in every human being, the inwardly, hidden aspect. And he comes with Esau together into this world by holding Esaus heel (thus his name ,Jacob', in Hebrew ,Ya'akov', translateable as ,hand on the heel'), that is: he arrives ,by a trick' only, he doesn't really ,belong here' from the perspective of this world, he does not really fit in, he is ,odd' (another translation of Ya'akov's name can be indeed ,he is bent, he is odd'). But exactly HE is the one, who gets the

,blessing of the Father' (although ,by a trick' again, from the worldly, ,logical' view), and who will finally become the archfather of the People of Israel. We will look at the important dynamics of the twin brothers Jacob and Esau again in more detail in the next part of this introduction, when meditating on the central sign of the five ,fruit signs': Gemini, the ,twins'.

4: netzach; Moses (Exodus 2,1-Deuteronomy 34,12); the mythical planet Mercury; ,the fire that is burning and consuming the wooden stick', the attempt to ,break the fruitless cycle' of cause and effect by means of a 'new breakthrough', but unlike the breakthrough ,out of nothing' of the very beginning as something completely new, now this breakthrough comes as a ,birth out of the present chaos', as something building up JUST out of the ,available' existing.

Moses, who is determined to rescue the ,Children of Israel' out of ,Egypt's Slavery', is tried to be killed by Pharao from the beginning on (see Exodus 1,16+22). But only BECAUSE of this try by Pharao, in the end Moses even is getting raised especially well (namely directly on the court of Pharao, as the step-son of Pharao's daughter; see Exodus 2,5-10).

The reason, why this ,Moses' is being hated everywhere he appears, is that he is the one saying: ,here is something wrong', when you are thinking, just now everything is perfect … That's why even his Israelite brothers are hating him again and again; sometimes not wanting to follow him any longer, sometimes even wanting to kill him. Moses brings a certain kind of ,restlessness' into the experience of

66

life, always pushing you to go further, to never be satisfied before having reached true freedom, to not make any foul compromises.

And by this fiery restlessness ‚Moses‘, as the Sephirah 'netzach‘, is ‚the victory‘; such a victory, which is so clear and definite, that there is not even the necessity to try hard, when you just KNOW that you are going to ‚win‘, to achieve this or that, because it is just ‚your thing‘.

5: hod; Aaron (Exodus 4,14-Numeri 20,29); the mythical planet Jupiter; ‚the water drowning the fire, which seems to be burning away the fruit‘, the material ‚barrier‘ of reality, which sets a boundary to the inspiration of human creativity, so that it won't ‚consume itself‘ in a rush; like in the play of the waters, in its streams of hotness dividing the cold masses of an ocean, sometimes heating up until condensation, and raining down again; by this the heat of the invisible fire becomes visible for us, ‚materializes‘.

After Moses has the inspiration, his brother Aaron expresses it, as the ‚Priest‘. Like always the ‚right side‘ is the breaking through, the hidden and abstract (the ‚male‘), and the corresponding ‚left side‘ is the causal consequence of it, the concrete and appearing revelation of the hidden source (the ‚female‘).

A ‚person‘ (or an aspect inside yourself) you meet in this sphere of ‚hod‘ is going to show you the connection between the horizontal and the vertical dimension, between the world of time and space and the acausal, surprising, miraculous impact from another realm into this world, and he is going to

67

show you that both belongs together, forms a unity.

Aaron is therefore being responsible for the orderly application of the ‚qurban‘, the ‚approach to God‘, the sacrifice of the ‚animal‘, the bodily existence, the ‚form‘, to make it a ‚praise (of God)‘ in the spiritual realm, too.

6: jesod; Joseph/’Zaphenath-Paneach‘ (Genesis 30,22-50,26); the mythical planet Venus; ‚the ox drinking the water to be nourished by it‘, the ‚animalistic‘ foundation of humanity being nourished especially by the ‚female‘, time-and-space side of existence, by the appearing, being tempted by it to choose THIS side instead of the spiritual, eternal.

The Hebrew word ‚jesod‘ means ‚foundation‘, but is also translateable as the sentence ‚it is a secret‘. So the (true) foundation (of anything in this world and of this world herself) is always a secret, otherwise it could not be the true foundation, but only one out of many ‚causes‘ in an infinite row of ‚cause-and-effect‘-relations inside this world.

The biblical character Joseph is ‚the misunderstood one‘, ‚the hated one‘ among the 12 brothers, being sold into slavery; but exactly by this ‚being-sold-away‘ he is becoming the de-facto-king of Egypt, getting his new name ‚Zaphenath-Paneach‘ by Pharao, as the one who is saving the whole world in a time of ‚great hunger‘. And beside this it is an important detail of this Sephirah that Joseph is from the beginning on the most loved son of the Father, being this without any ‚visible‘ reason, only, because his father ‚decided so‘.

7: malkhuth; David (1 Samuel 16,11 – 1 Kings 2,11);

68

the mythical planet Saturn; ‚the man slaughtering the ox, as the seemingly logical consequence to all the happenings around him', Mankind striving to ‚get rid of' but still ‚be nourished by' the own ‚animalistic', physical side of existence, as the seemingly ‚logical' consequence to the visible happenings in this material world we live in.

David is always in fight with someone. Even as the king of whole Israel there are still wars within or without his kingdom, never there is complete peace for him. The peace only comes after him, for his son Solomon (Sh'lomoh, meaning ‚peaceful; harmonic; fulfilled'), the ‚Son of David', representing the ‚8th day' finally.

Of course there is much, much more to these Sephiroth. Looking into the details of the biblical storylines of the corresponding characters can already bring forth many additional insights. And as soon as we look into the seven planets in part five, there will be clarified some more aspects of ‚the seven'. But on this first foundation now given above, we can finally begin to look at the three zodiacal signs of the male character, in their unity envisioning the ‚vertical way' out of this horizontal ‚world of the 4', of time and space (which is, as seen in the last part, illustrated by means of the four female signs of the Zodiac).

The first male sign is Virgo. The name means ‚virgin', or ‚young woman'; in Hebrew it is called ‚bethulah' (which equally means ‚young woman', especially in the sense, ‚woman, without having given birth to a child yet').

This sign taken as a ‚male' sign may seem irritating on the first glance, since it is an apparently female symbol for this male sign; but especially by this ‚contradiction' it correctly represents what could be called ‚the heavenly origin of the female'; that is: the heavenly origin of the earth, or ‚the male side of the female', the inner side of all the appearing world; it is picturing ‚the secret origin of the revealing and of the revealed'.

The christian symbol of the ‚Virgin giving birth to the Messiah' is to be understood in this sign: the Earth, the earthly realm, that is symbolically the ‚woman', ‚giving birth' to, or bringing forth the possibility of 'salvation', without being ‚impregnated' therefore by the forces of this world, but instead by being impregnated by the transcendent ‚male', by the ‚heavens', by the 'spirit'. It is nothing rational, nothing which could be achieved by the means of this world, by actively ‚working for it'. It is granted by the irrational, acausal side of reality – it just happens. And trying to explain the salvation in a definite way will always fail, or even will have the opposite effect: only drawing you deeper into the enslavement of the causal world, if you start feeling guilty for 'not understanding it', thinking, that your (supposed) ‚lack of insight' would be the reason for the absence of salvation in your life. But as long as we want to enforce this salvation by whatever ways, it always will be a ‚false Messiah' we are proclaiming, an ‚Antichrist' (= greek translation of ‚false Messiah'), as it is called in the (greek written) New Testament.

This ‚birth out of heavenly impregnation', and the

70

‚heavenly woman' necessary for it, though does not appear for the first time in the New Testament of the Bible. Often in the Old Testament already there are stories with ‚two wives', of which only the one of them is the ‚right one'. In these stories also ‚the other wife', the earthly one, may bring forth children, but not the ‚children of the promise'. The most famous of such stories is the story of Abraham and his two wives, the ‚Egyptian' woman and the ‚Hebrew' woman, called Hagar and Sarah (see Genesis chapter 16). From the ‚immanent woman', from Hagar – sure, from HER Abraham can instantly imagine to get a son, he believes THAT easily to be possible, when his actual wife, Sarah, is suggesting it, because that way would be quite 'normal'. But from Sarah herself, the ‚old one', the one ‚from the other side' (we remember: the word ‚Hebrew' means ‚from the other side', so: ‚heavenly'), from ‚the transcendent', so to speak?! That would be waaay too ‚miraculous' for Abraham … But yet there comes the son from Sarah, too: Isaac, or in Hebrew actually ‚Yitzchak', meaning ‚ridiculous', ‚laughable', or ‚incredible'. Because that's just what it is, when you experience this ‚virgin birth' in yourself, this ‚being impregnated by the heavenly': it is incredible, you can only laugh without explanation for it, no words seem appropriate anymore!

But the zodiacal sign of Virgo does not only represent this possibility of a ‚heavenly fruit' inside the earthly realm by means of ‚a miracle'. It also bears in itself the (often unconscious) remembrance of ‚the Garden Eden' (in Hebrew ‚gan eden'; literally meaning ‚a guarded realm of delight and pleasure'), of the Paradise of the beginning of Mankind. And with this

71

comes a deep longing, to reach that Paradise, ‚that beautiful Virgin' again. We can search in all cultures of this world, always we will find in one or another form a story of ‚the lost paradise', a state of life, which we lost, but which still is remembered (psychologically this phenomenon would probably be explained nowadays as ‚every individual's remembrance of the time in the mother's womb' …). And even the believe, that this lost paradise will be reached again at some point in the future, seems to be quite universal in all human cultures of history.

And for the sign of Virgo all this remembrance and hope is very important: in the sixth sign, as in the 6th day of creation week, Mankind is created; but Mankind ‚is falling' from their original state of delight, already on this 6th day, too. And in the sign Virgo (that means: in this layer of human nature) you somehow ‚know' (or ‚feel') about this human state of being, there is that feeling that Mankind is not ‚finished' yet, that we will only be complete(d) on the ‚8th day', in the coming world, which is not of this world we live in now, just like we do not have our origin in this world we live in now. From our 7th day-existence we look into our 6th day-creation and feel: we will arrive back there again, but it will be only ‚on the next day'.

So this sixth zodiacal sign is strongly associated with ‚Mankind' in its original state, in its state ‚meant to be'. And this Mankind can be seen as ‚the connection between Heaven and Earth', being the 'nail' connecting them both – Mankind indeed is like the word ‚and' in the formulation ‚Heaven AND Earth' (in Hebrew: 'sh'mayim WA aretz'); the ‚and' in

72

Hebrew is ‚wa‘, a word spelled only with the one letter ‚Waw‘. And this Hebrew letter Waw indeed resembles a nail in its original picture symbol, a ‚connecting device‘, and the word ‚waw‘ itself means ’nail‘, too. And Waw is the 6th letter of the Hebrew Alphabeth; the ’six‘ as the number of the day on which Mankind is created, and the ’six‘ as the base for the ’number of the beast, being the number of Man‘, the infamous ’sixhundredsixtysix‘, as it is mentioned in the last book of the Bible (Revelation 13,18), referring to an unholy state of being, where everything is reduced to this ’six‘, to this number of the beastly, earthly, only-human, of Egypt’s slavery, of an everlasting remaining in the ’sixth day‘ with its fall from Paradise, never coming into the ‚peace of the Sabbath day‘ and beyond.

Now, all this experience of the sign of Virgo would be very beautiful and without suffering, if the sign has kept its connection to the other two male signs, Libra and Scorpio, respective the connection to the 7th and 8th day. But when this connection is corrupted or completely lost, the Virgo-layer inside us feels a little bit like

Adam is said to have been feeling in the very first night he had to experience in his life: after being created in the day half of the 6th day (in Hebrew thinking the days begin with the night half), he is driven out of the Garden in the ‚late afternoon‘, shortly before the night would have approached. Thus, till then he never has known the darkness of the night. And now, when he experiences his first night, he is in indescribable fear of the darkness, because he of course cannot know yet, that this

73

darkness will come to an end in the morning again.

Such is the terror felt by the human being, when we are not knowing that there will be a recovery of the Paradise in the end, when we are fearing the death of the flesh, which is obviously approaching (we see this death all around us in this world), and think of this fleshly death as the ultimate end of us. Then we only can hope for some ‚false Messiah‘, for some pseudo-salvation in the shape of material wealth, social status or technological assistance for longer and healthier life. It would be like having the remembrance of that great promise to reach the Garden Eden of the origin again – but then realizing to be perishing in this world of time and space, without ever having reached that paradise again, with no other choice than to assume that the great promise will just be broken and never fulfilled.

A being in the Virgo sign HAS indeed in itself the salvation, but if it is separated from the other two days/signs like this, then the salvation cannot be realized in him/her for now, and that's of course tragic. He/She WILL still reach it in the end, no doubt; but until then it is a hard, an even cruel journey of life with much suffering. Suffering will be there anyways. Only, with the connection to the other two male signs, this suffering will be experienced as ‚the path‘, and by this as much less devastating.

The secret lies in the meaning of this suffering of ‚the lost sixth day‘: Like the olive HAS to be picked from the olive tree, to not decay on the tree. Then the olive HAS to be pressed to give its precious oil. And the ‚oil‘ then is, what is used for the ‚anointment‘, for the ‚anointed one‘ to become what he is; and the

74

,Anointed One' in Hebrew is the ,Mashiach', the ,Messiah' (or in Greek the ,Christ').

From this perspective on the oil and its importance for the Messiah as the bringer of salvation on the eighth day, it is not a surprise, that in the biblical list of ,the seven fruits of the promised land' (see Deuteronomy 8,8) the sixth of those fruits is the olive ... and that the Hebrew word for ,oil' is 'shaman', which is spelled with exactly the same letters like the word for the number ,8'!

Life in this world is traditionally compared to a candle (or an oil lamp): The picture of a burning down candle means: something which is disappearing here, is thereby appearing, even fulfilling itself ,on the other side'; so, if the candle burnt down here in this world completely, then it is present in its totality on the other side. The human being in the sign of Virgo COULD indeed experience his downfall, his ,burning down completely' in this world (when losing his connection to the 7th and 8th sign and day), but ... the meaning of life is NOT here in time and space!

In the Hebrew tradition the ,wheel' is the primary symbol for ,reincarnation', even the word for this concept (,gilgul') has to do with the word for wheel (,gal'): everything comes back again; not only that one little part of the wheel is ,real', that touches the ground at one moment in time, but ALL of the wheel is ,real' and even necessary for its purpose, and every little part of it will ,come again', get in touch again with the ground, just ,after another spin' ...

It is only the UNITY of the numbers 6, 7 and 8 (and

75

of the corresponding three male zodiacal signs) that bears in itself the 'secret of evil', the understanding of all the suffering; of the incomprehensible, which is there, so that there can be enlightenment, illumination in the dark, explanation for the enigmatic, answers to all the asking ,why?!' … Evil will not become ,Good' by understanding it. But it will become appreciated in a mysterious way nevertheless. In the Bible it is especially the book of ,Job' (or ,Iyob'), which elaborates on this insight.

In the sign of Virgo thus, the individual HAS to experience being heavily underestimated, in essential questions being thoroughly misunderstood, and in general remaining unrecognized in his/her true virtue and value by the world. But then again just this underestimatedness will be realized as a pathway to salvation, if you are still knowing nevertheless, that there is more about you, than the world can see. Then you will accept, that liberation can only be given to someone being captive before, that ressurection can only happen to someone having died before.

The situation of someone in the sign of Virgo, especially of someone who has lost the connection to the other two male signs, can be compared to one aspect of the situation of King Solomon in one famous tale, when that great and wise king has lost his ,ring of power', by which he used to have even the devil himself under his control: Suddenly he is not believed anymore to be the Son of David, the King of Jerusalem, and he has to go ,into exile'. But even at this lowest point in his life, HE himself still knows, although he cannot prove it to anyone: I AM the Son of David, the King of Jerusalem.

76

The danger of this sign of Virgo (beside the already mentioned separation from the other two male signs) is to be led astray by looking for your own power and strenght in the causal, in being ‚mighty in this world‘. You then will fall in a ‚too materialistic version of salvation‘ (which is NO true salvation) – IF you achieve anything at all. The way better advice for someone in this sign of Virgo is always to ‚draw yourself back‘, ’stay in the background‘, ‚just LET it happen‘ instead of ‚trying to MAKE it happen‘. You may want to compare this tendency to the female sign of Aries/Lamb, which would be on the horizontal level of the same characteristics in this regard.

The second male sign then is Libra, the ’scales‘. In its Hebrew name it is known as ‚meoznayim‘ (from the word for ‚balances‘; the word for ‚ears‘, ‚oznayim‘ is in it). It is the seventh sign in the visible circle of the Zodiac on the night sky.

It is said that the male sign of Libra is strongly connected to the female sign of Pisces; the main difference of the two lies in the opposition of ‚active and passive‘: Libra is the active counterpart of the passive Pisces, both though have intimately to do with ‚time‘, with ‚the water‘ in the mythical sense. While in Pisces the focus is on the ‚being fished out‘ of the water, in Libra that focus is on the ‚journey through‘ the same water; but more on the surface now, like on a boat manoeuvring through the waves, not as the fish swimming UNDER the water anymore.

And directly connected to the aforementioned, this seventh sign, and especially the ’seventh day‘ (of

‚creation week') associated with this sign, is understood as ‚the long way through the Wilderness', too, connecting the ‚Land of Egypt' (mitzrayim, numeric value of 380) with the promised ‚Land of Canaan' (khana'an, numeric value of 190), as the journey ‚from the 2 to the 1' (380 to 190 = 2 to 1), from duality back to unity, through ‚this world of time, space and matter', this world of the symbolical ‚water'. And, not-so-coincidentally, in the Hebrew Alphabeth the 7th letter is the Zayin, which is pictured originally as ‚a boat with a paddle', looked at from the side.

Libra thus is called ‚the sign of the way', ‚the sign of the path'. And especially the LONG way is meant here …

There is a certain verse in the biblical account of the exodus of the people of Israel out of Egypt (Exodus 13, 17), which is usually translated as something like: ‚And it came to pass when Pharao had let the people go, that God guided them not through the way of the land of the Philistines, although that was near, for God said: lest the people repent when they see war, and turn again to Egypt.'

But a far more literal translation would be: ‚[…] that God did not bestow on them the way of the land of the Philistines, because that (way) is near, and because God said: may the people not sigh by their vision of war, so that they (would) turn around back to Egypt.'

So the ‚way being near' is equated with a ‚vision of war'; and this understanding is taken by the ancient Hebrew tradition as an explanation, that ‚the way' in general HAS to be long for Mankind, because if everything is achieved in one single step, it would be ,way too much to take'.

For example: If we would see at once shortly before our birth into this world all the stuff we are going to eat during our whole life, it probably would make us … well, it could make us ,give up before trying', since it would appear to be sooooo indescribeable much and thus impossible to accomplish. So we need ,the long way', to get it done: one meal after another, never exactly knowing when the next meal will be, what exactly it will be; and in every single meal one spoon after another, chewing the food, swallowing it piece by piece, digesting it, and so on. And by this ,long way' it is no problem for us anymore to master that large amount of food during our whole life span.

Like concerning the food we eat during our lifetime, we should look at our life of this world in general like this: to just go step by step, not all the time worrying, ,how much food' it will be in total at the end, but to concentrate only on the little part of it visible just before us right now. And enjoy this little part right now as much as possible, being grateful for it, like we should be thanking for every meal we eat (see Deuteronomy 8,10).

It is said that ,the way itself knows, where it leads: there once was a paradise, we will be there again', that's it. So if we just trust the way we are walking on, everything will be alright. Thus the most important human capacity in this sign is: trusting patience.

The scales are envisioned as always ,balancing out',

but as never actually finding equilibrium with both sides being on the same level without any further movement. That equilibrium would be the end of the time world, there would be no journey anymore. So it goes always from one side to the other side, the left side representing the ‚evil‘, the doubt and desperateness, the right side representing the ‚good‘, the convincedness and the joy of having hope. And BOTH sides are essential to the joy in the long run:

It is like a true love story: first there is a falling in love, maybe even on the first sight. But then there is some drifting apart again sometimes, having some misunderstandings, very heavy ones even maybe. And disappointment. But then such misunderstandings are being solved again, and the joy is even bigger than it could have been without the temporary distancing in between. Up and down it goes in this sense, until finally there is a mutual commitment for each other, grown over time, as a decision both dare to make; after they know BOTH sides of the journey together, the sweet hours and days and weeks, but the tougher parts of this adventure, too. And then at some point a kind of engagement time begins, still learning about each other more and more, maybe during the first time of actual living together in one house, learning to accept the moments of needing some space for oneself, those moments of the other one and those moments of oneself, too, which may have been not expected as such in the beginning … But if both agree to all of this, ultimately ‚marriage‘ can ‚happen‘, there can be the ‚wedding‘ as a feast with all the family taking part, now with the general confidence that all is built on a true foundation indeed. Both, Man and Woman,

80

already knowing ABOUT each other so much, are finally ready to actually KNOW each other now – that is the ‚wedding‘ in the more intimate sense, happening in every new moment again and again.

And THIS wedding is, what mystically is said to be only happening ‚on the eighth day‘ – our whole journey through this seventh day is to be perceived as the ‚phase of engagement‘. Where true wedding is happening, the 8th day is here already for them.

In the Bible there are mentioned 7 specific ‚fruits of the Promised Land‘, which are interpreted in the tradition as ‚the 7 ways of growth‘. These 7 (+1) ‚fruits‘ of the Promised Land (see Deuteronomy 8, 8) are: Wheat, Barley, Grape, Fig, Pomegranate, Olive, Date (respectively the ‚honey‘ of dates) and, as the eight (but not mentioned in this specific scripture), Almond. If we see these seven fruits as corresponding to the seven days of creation (and to the 7 Sephiroth, etc.), we have the Date as the fruit of the 7th day, of ‚our time-and-space-world‘. And the Hebrew word for this fruit (and for the tree on which it grows) is ‚thamar‘; a word meaning not only ‚date (palm tree)‘, but it can be translated as the sentence ’she is bitter‘, too. So our ’seventh day‘ down here, and our journey through it, is associated with ‚bitterness‘; the world, in her horizontal, female character of ‚time, space and matter‘, is regarded as being something ‚bitter‘. But still as the ‚date‘, as the ’sweetest fruit of all‘ …

Finally, it is said, ‚in the end of the journey‘, the scale is ‚down on the right‘ and has reached the end of our 7th day. Then the transition to the coming world is experienced, to the world of the ‚eighth day‘, the promised world, which all the way along has been granting the meaning, the sense of our whole journey.

If you search for the lost Paradise in the historic past of this world of time, or hope for it as ‚coming back‘ in the future of this world of time, then you are ‚cutting off the seventh day from the two days before and after it‘, separating it out of its connection to the whole. And that necessarily leads to suffering and disappointment, just like the separation of the 6th day from the two following. When someone only sees this ‚underestimatedness‘ of his/her person, only feels unrecognized, not knowing yet, that exactly this underestimatedness will be his/her way to salvation through this current seventh into the promised 8th day. Expecting this 8th day as such, already reachable in THIS world, would mean to not see the ‚waters‘ which have to split first, always when you come ‚from one day to the next‘; like at the exodus from the land of Egypt into the Wilderness you have to pass through the Red Sea (in Hebrew: ‚yam suph‘, meaning ‚Sea of the End‘ or ‚Sea of the Border‘), and then from the Wilderness into the Promised Land you have to pass through the Jordan river (in Hebrew ‚yarden‘, meaning ‚descendance; going/falling down‘).

The Libra-layer in every human being is very strongly looking and searching for a target, for sense and meaning, for a final aim of the journey. With this goes motivation and the already mentioned ‚trusting patience‘ on the one (the ‚right‘) side, but the disappointment, too, on the other (the ‚left‘) side, when we sometimes cannot see anything supporting our hopes for reaching the promised at the end, when we feel deceived, be it ‚by God', or be it ‚by our own illusions'. But all this is part of this sign, and when we accomplish to reconnect to the 6th and the 8th sign, too, in this sign of Libra, then we will never be suffering a pain unbearable, but at most a pain experienced ‚for the sake of the adventure', so to speak …

Because on the long way through the Wilderness of this world, sometimes there IS doubt, sometimes we ARE rebellious like Israel in the desert, longing back to Egypt with all its 'security', with all its ‚tasty dishes'. But we realize, too, at some point that: once freed from slavery, it is not anymore possible to actually go back: ‚Egypt would spit you out!' it is said … ‚even if you would offer yourself as a slave again'. Once liberated, you can PERISH – but you cannot ever go back to enslavement again …

The ‚Wilderness', or ‚desert', in the Hebrew language is called ‚midbar'. The interesting aspect of this Hebrew word is, that it can also mean ‚conversation' (from the root word ‚debar', meaning ‚word; speaking'). So the whole journey of this seventh day, our experience in this world of the '40 years of wandering through the wilderness', this world of time and space, is perceived as one great ‚conversation'. And in this sign of Libra, the scales balancing itself out with alternate movements to the left and to the right, this ‚conversation' is sketched as having a specific character: the conversation namely always ‚takes its turns' with the conversing parties, it never should be in a complete equilibrium, 'standing still', but should be a constant moving ‚to and fro' (just like the scales is pictured, as always being on one side weightier than on the other).

The third male sign of the Zodiac is Scorpio, the 'scorpion', in Hebrew named ‚aqrav' (equally meaning 'scorpion', or in a certain context ‚a specific kind of whips with stings on it', see 1 Kings 12,11).

Like it is typical for every ‚third' in a row, the third ‚male sign' of the Zodiac, too, is of a ‚twin character', of dual nature (compare for instance to the third of the female signs we already discussed in the second part of this introduction, Pisces, which is the ‚two fish'-symbol; and also to the third sign in the whole Zodiac circle, which is the sign of Gemini, ‚the twins', and which at the same time is the third of the five ‚fruit signs', too; beside this, in the accounts on the ‚creation week', we also find the dual nature of the third at least twice, in the happenings of the third and of the sixth day).

So beside the name 'scorpion' this sign is called ‚(white) eagle', too (in Hebrew 'nesher'). The aqrav/nesher-dualism represents the Anti-Christ and the Christ; ‚Devil and God'.

We already mentioned that the Hebrew word for the number eight is spelled with exactly the same letters as 'shaman', meaning the ‚anointing oil', which is the characteristic sign of the ‚Messiah' (since ‚messiah'/'mashiach' means ‚anointed one'). And we already learned that the oil for this anointment stems from the ‚olives pressed on the 6th day'.

But what exactly is the ‚eigth day', when looking at it from our world of time and space with the 'seven-day-week', the ‚four-week-month' and the ‚twelve-

84

month-year'? Is it the so-called 'sunday', the day after the seventh day, so just the first day of the week again? No, not really. Because actually there is a ‚hidden' 8th day, namely ‚the rest that remains' in a lunar month after the 4 weeks of 7 days, so after the 28 days of 4 ‚regular' weeks; the 1.5 days, which ‚do not fit in' into the scheme of a four-week-month. This 'non-fitting rest' can be compared to the 10 days of the solar year, which are exceeding the 355 days of the 12 lunar months, making a '13th zodiacal sign' partly visible in this difference of days between the lunar and solar cycle (indeed ‚modern' astronomy speaks of this 13th zodiacal sign, too, calling it the 'snake bearer').

In these seemingly ‚irrational rests' we can observe that in our world of time and space there is always an incalculateable irrational factor, despite all the ‚laws' and all the ‚causality'. Trying to ignore this always-present ‚rest' means ignoring reality, means trying to suppress reality under our own human will, thus essentially ‚reaching for the throne of God' as the legitimate ruler of this creation …

The 'scorpion' is in the tradition always associated with the 'serpent', the 'snake' from the beginning in the Garden, and furtherly equated with the mythical ‚dragon', which is no other than the ‚devil' itself, the one who ‚brings doubt', who 'splits everything apart'; and another important name of this being is of course 'satan', meaning ‚adversary; hinderer, inhibitor' (see for example Revelation 20,2). He is the ‚Anti-God' of this world of time and space; when we are looking for the ultimate reason and source of the material world, at some point this mythical

,dragon' shows up, dressed up as ,god', to deceive the seeking one into worshipping him as the ,understandable' source of everything – instead of finding the invisible and incomprehensible TRUE Creator by the actual experience of Him.

The other side of this zodiacal sign is the (white) Eagle, ,bringing his young ones on his wings with him' (these ,young ones' are – as strange as it may sound – actually ,the dove', which is the symbol for the ,message out of heaven'). The Eagle alone is only exactly as strong as the dragon is, just with a strenght and power coming from the opposite direction. So there would be no decision, no winner, no loser in a confrontation, since both are equal. But by the little additional power through ,the dove', the Eagle is going to be victorious anyways!

A ,fight' in the Hebrew mode of thinking always means a ,knowing each other'. That is, you shall get to know your enemy, as well as he shall get to know you through the confrontation. Otherwise it would be not a real fight, only a unilateral suppression, a violation. From this perspective it is not possible, to only ,know the dragon (or serpent, or scorpion)', without letting him know YOU, too. If that one-sided-ness is tried nevertheless (that you learn about the satan, without letting him know about you, too), the dragon will probably break out in even more furious anger, because you denied him ,his right', he would have ,justice on his side' then.

In the Hebrew tradition it is said: In a teacher-student relation there shall never be an imbalance between the personal knowledge of the two sides of each other. So, the teacher cannot know about all of the personal situation of his student, while staying an ‚anonymous dark shadow' himself. Such an imbalance would be called ‚fornication'.

In the end, the Eagle in this sign always is victorious over the Scorpion. But still: always there remains the possibility of the Devil to ‚get free again', because he only gets captured, incarcerated, but never destroyed completely (this aspect can be compared to the famous ‚Achill's heel' of the greek mythology, too).

A typical ‚Scorpio-experience' is told as the famous tale of ‚King Solomon and his Powerful Ring', which we already referred to several times now during the course of this introduction. It goes like this:

When King Solomon is at the height of his power, reigning over the whole Nation of Israel in a peaceful time without any wars, having built the first Temple of God and keeping good friendly relations to all the mighty neighboring kingdoms, he even has the devil himself under his control: by means of a powerful ring on his finger, wherein the name of God is engraved, he has forced the devil into chains and keeps him in front of his throne.

Then one day the devil, appellating to Solomons mercy, convinces the King to give him the ring once for only a second, so that he may feel for a moment how it feels to have such power. ‚I am in chains anyways, so I cannot do anything!' he says … So Solomon agrees, out of compassion with ‚that poor devil' … The devil gets the ring into his hands – and directly throws it out of the window into the sea, where it sinks to the ground and cannot be found anymore.

By this happening, Solomon loses all his power, the devil takes his throne and is reigning as the king of Jerusalem now, because nobody actually looks at the person on the throne, but just respects the throne itself as the symbol of authority. So the whole People of Israel is serving the devil in these times, without anyone except for Solomon knowing it. Salomon himself tries to prove that HE is the real king, the actual Son of David, but the people won't believe him, they even want to throw him in jail for claiming to be the king. Salomon thus flees the country, and it is said, in this situation he is writing the biblical book of ‚koheleth' (‚Ecclesiastes'), wherein the author always refers to the ‚meaningless world' he experiences with the famous words ‚vanity of vanities, all is vanity' …

In his ‚exile', the unrecognized Solomon is working as a cook at the court of a certain foreign king. And in this notion of ‚being a cook', there is a Hebrew play on words: A cook is someone, who prepares the meals and puts them on the table of people. The Hebrew word for ‚meal' or ‚dish' is 'seuda', a word related to the word 'sod', meaning 'secret, mystery'. And then ‚that meal' is put on the ‚table', which would be the Hebrew word 'shulchan', translateable also as ‚that which is sent'. So the ‚cook preparing the meal on the table' is ‚the one (relatively unrecognized) figure in life, who is preparing the secret on what is sent for you', or more simplified: ‚the one who is creating the mystery of your destiny' …

The tale goes on then: Solomon marries a daughter of

the king he is working for. Of course that king is not amused by the news of that wedding (‚What? A cook?! No way, don't even think about it, or I will have him executed!') … so they both run away and marry against the will of her father. On Solomons next working place, again as a cook, he is preparing a fish. And when he opens the belly of that fish, he finds inside it … his Magic Ring! Instantly he sits on his throne in Jerusalem, and the devil is bound in his chains again, under complete control by the re-established King.

So, Solomons journey around the world as ‚the unrecognized' is indeed easily to identify as a typical ‚Scorpio-experience': The ‚Achill's heel' of Solomon in this tale is his mercy, his compassion, even with the devil himself. Without this mercy, the chained devil would have never got free again. But then there would have been no 'story' either. And there would have been no book of ‚Ecclesiastes', nor the daughter of that one king would have married the Son of David, nor Solomon would have ever experienced ‚the other side' of life in this world (being raised as a king from the beginning, he never had to suffer the pain of ‚ordinary man', so to speak). Now he knows. And maybe … by this experience he is now even happier and stronger than before.

We can compare these dynamics to the events in the Garden of Eden, where the (necessary) fall of mankind is induced by the Snake (= Scorpion/Dragon), making Mankind to ‚go to another (lower/deeper) level', to be able to experience the joy of ‚coming home again' in the end. In this sense, the whole unity of the three male signs, of the 6th, 7th

and 8th day of creation, is illustrated in this tale of King Solomon losing his Ring of Power and getting it back in the end. And it is giving another clue: there is not reached the ultimate end yet, when having reached the 8th day (as Solomon had reached that 8th day, having built the Temple of God here on Earth, reigning over the whole united Israel in peaceful times) … the devil still has to break out once again (see the book of Revelation, too, concerning this ‚last outbreak‘, chapters 20,3+7-10).

A human being in this sign of Scorpio WANTS this confrontation with the ‚Evil‘, needs it, because he/she wants to know himself by knowing the whole world, including the very most evil, the ‚devil‘. The danger here is, to become ‚totalitarian‘ in character, wishing to control the whole surrounding world. But in the better case this ‚totalitarianism‘ only has the effect, that you are just seeing everything around yourself as relevant for your own life, and by this you are feeling very closely connected to all the surrounding world, as if she is a part of yourself.

It is all about having this great fight in YOURSELF, to stand in the end before God, perceiving the insight, as being whispered to you from out of the heavenly realms: ‚that is YOU‘. Although without thinking of yourself to BE ‚God‘, of course; but you are seeing yourself finally ‚in the resemblance of God‘, how God even is IN you, to share all your experience with you, your suffering as well as your joy, and by this you are realizing now how deep the responsibility is, which comes with that experience of being made in resemblance of the Eternal One.

As already hinted at, something important is realized in this last of the male signs: On the 8th day ‚only‘ the individual salvation is realized! The 9th and 10th day follow, where the ‚Whole‘ gets finally saved for the coming world, too. The 9th after it appears and is experienced as the (journey through the) ‚underworld‘, which is revealed then, as actually being a ‚womb‘, a ‚matrix‘, from which the ‚New Heaven and New Earth‘ are being born out of. And the 10th day finally is the actual ‚future‘, the final stage of the development beginning with the ‚1‘, the unity of the origin, the ‚Oneness of Creator and Creation‘: the ʼ10‘ now being the ʼnew One‘, the One of the origin, now on a higher level: the ‚One in the Tens‘. But the details of these stages AFTER the 8th day, and their respective challenges, are content of the so-called ‚fruit signs‘ of the Zodiac, which will be described in the next part of this introduction.

In the tradition we can find an elaboration on the fact that King Solomon at some point marries Pharao's daughter (1 Kings 3,1). This marriage is counted as the particular decisive ʼsin‘, which has as its result the rise of the mythical ‚Roman Empire‘ (‚When Solomon married Pharaoh's daughter, [the archangel] Gabriel descended and stuck a reed in the sea, which gathered a sand-bank around it, on which was built the great city of Rome‘; stated in the Talmud at Sanhedrin 21b), as well as the destruction of the Temple of God, and even the split of the kingdom during the reign of Solomon's son Rehoboam (see 1 Kings 11,9-13 and 12,15ff).

Especially the split of the Solomonian kingdom after his death is interesting now in this sign of Scorpio.

The situation then is: two kingdoms, Judah and Israel; the 2 tribes of Judah and Benjamin forming the House of Judah in the southern kingdom, the 10 remaining tribes forming the northern kingdom called ‚Israel‘ or sometimes referred to as the ‚House of Joseph‘ or as ‚Ephraim‘ (named after the biggest tribe of the ten northern tribes, which originates from the descendants of the younger son of Joseph with the name Ephraim).

The one of the two kingdoms, Judah, is being ruled by one family dynasty (that of King David and his son Solomon), the other, Ephraim, being ruled by changing families; in Ephraim only rarely a son or grandson of the king becomes his successor, most of the times there are coups and rebellions leading to changes in the reign and by this, often completely new strongmen come to power in the kingdom of the North, that one of the ‚Ten Tribes‘, of ‚Josef‘, or ‚Ephraim‘.

And in the biblical accounts of the histories of the two kingdoms there is written about much more ‚evil‘, much more ‚rebelling against God’s commandments‘ in the northern kingdom, than there is reported about such in Judah. But still: God loves them both as his ’sons‘ and wants them to be finally reunited. This shows: the standards of judgement are not the same for God, as they would be for us, as the limited beings we are.

This ‚reunification of the two kingdoms‘ is the topic of the prophet Ezechiel’s visions of the ‚two sticks of wood‘ (actually ‚trees‘) with the names ‚Judah‘ and ‚Joseph‘ on them, becoming ONE Tree again, as a further explanation of Ezechiel’s earlier vision of

92

,many human bones, collected together to skeletons, growing flesh and skin again, being raised up and then being inspired by the wind, by the spirit, to live again'. It is the dead kingdom of Israel/Ephraim (the physical part, without the spiritual realm inside itself; historically present in virtually every nation of the Earth, because the '10 lost tribes of Israel' are said to be 'scattered among all the nations', having forgotten their true origin) enlivened by the other kingdom, by Judah (the spiritual part, lost its body, wandering around in the whole wide world without a true homeland on earth, but having strongly kept its identity and self-consciousness, as ,the wandering Jew').

Both these kingdoms are a reality INSIDE every human being, since inside ourself this very split – into the causal, material, so-called ,real' world on the one side (,Ephraim'), and then the realm of ,fantasy', ,imagination' and the ,only' mythical experience of believing and dreaming on the other side, ,where the Temple of God used to be present in Jerusalem' (,Judah') – has happened. The split in all of us has happened, only to cope with the ,outer world' around us, which has in herself established this split, too, and which won't accept any individual openly 'not accepting', or ,putting back together' this split …

So the reunification of the two kingdoms is still a matter of ,prophesy', of the future, at least concerning Mankind as a whole. Every single individual on the other hand of course HAS the chance in this life to experience this reunification of Judah and Israel. Because ,in the Bible there is no before and no after', how it is said. It is all eternal, every single story in it is happening in every single moment in every single soul.

But when dealing with it from the perspective of the Zodiac, this 'reunification of the two kingdoms' is accomplished only in the 'fruit signs'. As long as there is the opposition between 'male' and 'female' signs, we cannot have the RE-unified 'Israel under the reign of the (ETERNAL) Messiah' – we then have only that first unified Israel of Solomon, which he already 'inherited' from the 'Beloved One' ('Dawid' means 'beloved one') as a unity, being himself only a 'Son of David' (which is a traditional name of the expected Messiah – but only ONE name of him, another one is 'Son of Joseph', that is: the ETERNAL Messiah is of the '10 lost tribes', too …). So the RE-unification of the split kingdom is a matter of the 10th day …

To come to an end of this part dealing with the three 'male signs' of the Zodiac: It is essential that the 3 are understood in their belonging-together as a 'One', so that the equation is: 4 female signs plus 1 united male sign = the '4-1-principle' as 'the fruit', the 5 (as the number of the 'fruit signs' of the Zodiac). That means, in this regard there are in total 10 signs, instead of 12, illustrating thus the journey through all the 'ten days', too, instead of only the journey through the 'seven' of our world into the 'eight' of the world to come. But more to this in the following part.

To summarize at this point the main difference between male and female signs: The male signs are representing challenges, which play out themselves mainly through the INNER life of a human being, not

94

affecting the outside world with her concrete happenings in individual life (or the perception thereof) directly, as the female signs do it primarily. The male signs thus are dealt with as an individual much more ‚actively‘, compared to the more passive approach the individual has to take to the female signs‘ challenges. The ladder are in the contrary THEMSELVES actively coming onto the human being by means of the surrounding reality which is experienced and not so easily to be ignored or avoided. The former, the male signs, though contrarily have to be searched and found first in the OWN depths of inner experience, before they can have an (indirect) effect on the outside world, too.

It is the so-called ‚fruit signs‘, which will be topic of the following part of this introduction, where the male and female signs‘ opposite characteristics regarding this ‚active-or-passive-ness‘ ultimately are reaching a ’synthesis‘ in the individual experience of reality; then finally both, inside AND outside reality, are grasped as ONE whole.

The Third of the 3 Groups of the Zodiacal Signs: the 5 Fruit/Child Signs

As it has been explained already in the very first part of this introduction to Hebrew Astrology, the 'number 5' in the Ancient Wisdom represents the principle of the ‚child', of the ‚fruit' coming out of the confrontation, out of the ‚getting to know each other' of the principles of ‚male' and ‚female', 3 and 4. So it is no surprise that there are exactly five ‚fruit signs' in the Zodiac according to the Hebrew perspective on it. They are the remaining five: Capricorn, Sagittarius, Gemini, Cancer and Leo. In this order they are typically discussed in the ancient literature, so they appear (contrary to the male, as well as contrary to the female signs) NOT in a continuing row of the visible circle of the 12 signs on the sky: the 10th and 9th sign serve as the first two, then the 3rd, 4th and 5th of the 12 serve as the rest of them, as the 3rd, 4th and 5th of the 5. Thus we can say: they are 'split apart' by the male signs on the one side and by the female signs on the other. This can be interpreted as an expression of the fact that ‚the child is integrating both parents within itself'; and by this look on it, the WHOLE circle of the 12 signs represents the ‚fruit', the ‚Child of God'.

Sometimes indeed the 12 signs are grouped in the shape of a human being to symbolize that ‚primordial man' (called the ‚Adam Qadmon' in Hebrew), Mankind as it is created in the image and resemblance of God, filling out the whole cosmos with its appearance.

An interesting question for every horoscope is:

Which sign-group (male, female, fruit) is predominant? That means: Which way of experiencing the Eternal is more, and which is less typical for the human being under this constellation?

The ‚female' is experienced as that which is there around yourself, as the ‚outward destiny', but including also very individual factors like your body, your genes, etc.

The ‚male' is experienced as that which is to be found furthermost INSIDE yourself, it is your ‚inward destiny', coming from out of your own soul into your experience of life (of course of ‚outward life', too) and cannot be explained in any way purely by your physical situation and your surrounding world – it is the more ‚acausal'.

Now, the ‚fruit' then is experienced specifically as that which is 'not there yet' (in your natural state of being), neither around you, nor inside you, but what you long for (consciously or unconsciously or subconsciously) as the solution for all the contradictions of your inward and your outward perception of life, the solution to the personal conflicts between your experiences and your wishes.

The first of the fruit signs, Capricorn, depicts a certain kind of ‚male goat'. Its Hebrew name is ‚gedi' (= ‚male goat', too). There are only three animals of the Zodiac, which can serve as 'sacrifice', ‚qurban' in the biblical rite: those with horns on their heads; namely Taurus, Aries and Capricorn. As the third of those three animals with horns in the circle of the 12, Capricorn has a very ‚dual' character, as it is typical for any ‚third in a row', according to the

97

Ancient view on things.

Its ‚two sides‘ are especially illustrated in the ‚two goats for Yom Kippur‘ (see Leviticus 16,5-34), the biblical feast called ‚Day of Atonement‘. In the rite of this feast there is one goat to bring for the Eternal One as a ‚qurban‘ (we already know, this means: ‚for the approach towards the Eternal‘, ‚to come close to God‘), and one other goat there is which is destined ‚for Azazel‘. We will see, who or what this so-called ‚Azazel‘ is. And an important fact in the rite of this Day of Atonement is: the decision, which one of the two goats is going to be used for what purpose, is made by ‚the lot‘, by fortune, by ‚coincidence‘, not by any ‚rational choice‘.

Actually every single one of the 12 zodiacal signs has a basic structure of ‚two sides opposing each other‘, and these two sides of each sign somehow ‚want to get to know each other‘ inside the human being.

But in some of the signs, this opposition of two sides is especially prominent (for example in Scorpio and as we will see soon, in Gemini, too; but also for example in Pisces and in Libra; as mentioned before, actually always then, when the sign is in some kind of ‚third position‘ of a row). In Capricorn this oppositional character is very prominent.

In the aforementioned biblical feast of ‚Yom Kippur‘ and its rituals this double-character is described in the mythical pictures of the Ancients. This feast is a ‚day of atonement‘, a day of expiation – so a day of a crucial decision, where something ‚old‘ ends, and something ’new‘ is born. It is happening expressively ‚on the tenth day of the year‘.

98

To understand this in its significance, we have to take a broader perspective on this fact. The biblical year has two beginnings: One is the beginning of the (counting of the) months, which is around spring time, and which remembers the ‚Exodus‘, the liberation of the People of God out of the enslavement by ‚Egypt‘, by ‚this world of duality‘. The other beginning of the year is in autumn, and it is what is traditionally called the ‚day of creation of Mankind‘. This date in the calendar is actually 2 days, because of the new-moon-sighting marking the beginning of the new month, which is not predictable exactly, so it is celebrated on the two days which both could be the sighting dates. And it is said regarding this double dating of ‚New Year‘: Mankind has two origins, too: one in the visible, one in the invisible; like the new moon is twice to be dated, once in the still invisible, only ‚abstractly‘, and then again in the ‚concrete‘, when it is actually visible for the human eye in the evening sky. This date of ‚Creation of Mankind‘ is placed in the 7th month (counted from the remembrance month of the exodus out of Egypt), like it is the beginning of the 7th DAY, when (fallen) Mankind is appearing in this world of time and space, ‚outside the Garden of Eden‘ now.

So on this 10th day of the 7th month the ‚Day of Atonement‘ is celebrated, which is paradoxically nevertheless counted as the '10th day of the year‘, because biblically there are these two beginnings of the year, like there are the two beginnings of Mankind – and maybe also because there are for every human being two ‚beginnings of life‘: the first, 'natural‘ birth, corresponding to the ‚Creation of

Mankind'; and the second, spiritual birth, that ,being born again' which Jesus talks about as necessary for Salvation, for ,entering the Heavenly Kingdom' (see for example John 3,3ff), and this rebirth being equated with the 'spiritual liberation out of Egypt' in every individual life.

In the end of this Day of Atonement, the death of the individual is symbolized by certain rituals (especially in Judaism; the biblical recommendation is not so specific in this regard, only advises to ,humiliate one's soul' for the whole day, which is traditionally interpreted as a strict fasting without any food or drink for 25 hours). And the 'new life', with now ,all the sins having been taken away', having been ,expiated', through the atonement on this day, begins afterwards with the sound of the 'shophar', the ram's horn, which is used as a blowing instrument.

In the Ancient Wisdom ,the 10 always is an ending AND a new beginning': The 10th sign of the Zodiac is the beginning of the five fruit signs, while it is the last of the three ,horned animals' of the Zodiac. As already said: those ,horned animals' are the animals which can be brought as ,qurban', as sacrifice in the biblical rite (beside birds; but birds play an outstanding role in the biblical qurban-system anyways, since they are the only qurbans which are not ,cut into pieces', but stay WHOLE while serving as qurban).

And to make one thing clear once again at this point: ,qurban' is NOT a mass-slaughtering of animals, it is something happening ONLY in the ,mythical realm', in the ,Temple of God' (and ONLY there CAN it happen, this is indeed an explicit command in the

100

Bible! See Leviticus 17,2-5; Deuteronomy 12,11+13+14). And the ‚Temple' is present only in (mythical) ‚Jerusalem' (by the way, a word which can be translated as ‚city of peace' or as ‚His project of peace'), which is in that part of the 'split kingdom' (‚Judah'; see last part of this introduction), which represents the ‚only' imaginative side of reality, the ‚dream- and myth-side' of human experience, the so-called ‚unreal'.

It is our ‚longing for the silent, ineffable origin of ourselves', which actually means ‚qurban', the ‚approaching towards God', as ‚the other side' of experience. That is the reason, why the ‚Temple', the ‚House of God', the ‚Dwelling of the Eternal' (which would be the more literal translation of the Hebrew word for ‚Temple' in the Bible), is not in THIS world to find, it is ‚the place', NOT present in our world of 'space'. Indeed, the word for ‚place' (in Hebrew ‚ha maqum', literally ‚THE Place') is used as one specific 'name of God', because the true and whole essence of any ‚place' in this world of our perception is in reality far more than what we can perceive in this world of space. The place we see HERE is only the 'surface of the true PLACE', which is God Himself, always being present anywhere, if you will.

But with that longing for the 'silent origin', which we feel to be ‚in another realm' than this world of time and space – with that longing comes another urge inside us, namely the belief that there MUST be something more about THIS world here, too: the idea that maybe the secret we are looking for in the longing for our heavenly origin, indeed is concealed also in THIS world already. Because we can feel, we sense: THIS world, too, bears a certain inner secret; couldn't it be that this inner secret of hers is the same, as the one we are searching for on that ‚other side‘?! Indeed, the ‚far distant‘, we are longing for, could be much closer than we think sometimes … it could be HERE already!

It is again like in the so-called 'sacrifice of Isaac‘, when Abraham is called to sacrifice his one beloved son, of whom he was told that HE it shall be, who is going to inherit the land which was ‚promised to Abraham and his seed‘. And now the same God that promised this, wants Abraham to sacrifice this son?! It is obviously a paradox. But this IS how this world in our human experience works, it IS paradox.

Wouldn't it be nice if anything was easy, if we all would understand each other, nobody would ‚wear masks‘ anymore?

But that is not how it is; we do NOT understand each other perfectly all the time. Not at all. We all are strangers to each other, no matter how much we desire to know someone and BE known by someone. This paradox of our existence in this world will sustain. It HAS to sustain.

But let's get back to the qurban of the goat on ‚Yom Kippur‘: as already mentioned, the goat is a symbol for 'something coming to an end‘. In the Bible an ‚end‘ is typically characterized by the word ‚good‘ (most famous: see Genesis 1,4+10+12+18+21+25: ‚and God saw that it was good‘). In Hebrew the word ‚good‘ is ‚tov‘ and has a numeric value of 17, just like ‚gedi‘, the ‚male goat‘ and the name of the sign of Capricorn.

102

Besides this, the ‚Great Flood' happens in the 17th century after creation, Joseph is sold into slavery at the age of 17 (and, to deceive their father Jacob, Josephs brothers are imitating the blood on his garment with the blood of a slaughtered GOAT), and in the oral tradition there are several more 'seventeens' marking an end of one phase and the beginning of a new one.

So to summarize it: The 10th is always announcing an end, which then is expressed as ‚the 17'. And always it is a new beginning, too.

So now, ‚on the 10th day of the year', in the ‚mythical realm' these two goats are brought to the ‚House of God', to the ‚dwelling of the Eternal'. For the human being it is the searching and longing for an ‚end' (of ‚all the struggle'), but on the other hand it is a consciousness of an ‚ending' of oneself to be experienced, a knowledge of the finiteness of yourself. It is the so-called ‚end of times' so often spoken of in the Bible. But this does not mean some ‚ending of a linear time' at some point in the (far or near) future, but it means the ending of EVERY moment, of every hour, of every day; it is the never ending, everlasting end of ALL we experience in time. As humans, we always 'stand at the boundary' between past and future.

The human being in the sign of Capricorn is very aware of this fact, that ‚the (single) moment is crucial'. But again, crucial in a duality: on one hand the longing for the Eternal, for God; on the other the tendency towards the evil, the ‚devil': the other goat goes to ‚Azazel' – how it is described in the Bible for

103

the ritual on this special ‚day' of the '10th of the
Year', respectively the '10th of the 7th, (see Leviticus
16,20-22).

So ... Who is ‚Azazel'?? We can look at a little tale,
wherein this name appears: the tale of the rebellion of
some of the angels at the time of the creation of Man.
In this story ‚Azazel' (beside one other angel called
‚Semchasi') is one of the two leading angels of the
rebellion.

It is the point during the process of creation, where
God decides to create the original Mankind,
‚Primordial Man', also known as ‚the Son of Man',
the actual Human in his perfect origin as the
‚Messiah' for the whole of creation, the ‚One'
destined for the mission to ‚bring back home all the
manifoldness of nature' to the ‚Father's House' (see
part one of this introduction). As such, as the literal
‚Son of God', this primordial Mankind is perfectly
resembling their Heavenly Father.

It is like ‚the image of God painted by God himself
into the cosmos' – maybe indeed in the shape of the
Zodiac, but not yet as ‚the circle' as on our night sky
today, but still ordered in the form of a human being,
with head, body, arms and legs (the traditional image
is built up of: Aries and Taurus as the head, Gemini
making the arms, Cancer the chest with Leo as the
heart inside it, Virgo as the upper belly, Libra in the
middle of the whole body around the navel, Scorpio
as the loins area with the genital organs, Sagittarius
as the two upper legs, Capricorn the knees, Aquarius
the lower legs and Pisces the feet; so the circular
form of the 12 signs of nowadays is a symptom of

104

this ‚Adam Qadmon‘ being shattered into pieces and scattered amongst the whole firmament as a consequence of his ‚falling down from the spiritual realm into this world of matter‘ …).

So, this original Man has such a high status, as the ‚crown of creation‘, without having done anything himself yet for being granted this honour. This becomes the reason, why some ‚angels‘ (that is: ‚messengers of God‘) get jealous, they do not believe, the Man will appreciate this great gift of being made out of the divine love in the perfect resemblance of the Creator Himself, so that Mankind will be ungrateful. In other words: these angels believe, it would be ‚a bad decision of God‘, to create this Mankind at all.

Those angels also somehow represent a movement ‚inside the soul of God Himself‘, given that they are themselves created beings of Him, so not actually ‚independent‘. In this sense, it is God Himself, who ‚has His doubts‘ when creating Mankind. But nevertheless He does it, and the effect is that these angels ‚rebel‘ against this decision of the Almighty, and by this, they become a ‚hindering force‘, the universal ‚adversary power‘ in all creation, the so-called 'satanic‘, or in the more mythical wording: they become the ‚Fallen Ones‘, angels which ‚fell down from Heaven to Earth for having lost their right to stay up there‘.

Now the method of these fallen angels to sabotage the creation of Mankind is just to ‚teach‘ the human beings certain things … indeed the Fallen Ones are doing nothing else, than to ‚explain everything‘. We can obviously compare this to the 'snake-story‘ of the

Paradise, where the temptation of the ‚female‘ (= the bodily) side of Mankind, to ‚eat the forbidden fruit‘, is achieved by promising ‚to open their eyes‘.

‚Satan‘ himself is known in the tradition as ‚the angel which has been thinking too much‘. In the Hebrew the word for ‚thinking‘ is the exact same word as ‚calculating‘. And the problem of too much thinking and calculating and planning is: it makes it impossible to actually EXPERIENCE, what is being thought about! And exactly this law it is, which the fallen angels are well aware of, and they use it against us, until nowadays, holding us captive in an imaginary world of abstract thinking (or at least they are trying to do so).

By the way, it is also said: the fight of these angels against the decision of God, to create Mankind nevertheless, in spite of the possibility that Mankind will be ungrateful and not understanding the great love of their Creator – this ‚angelic rebellion‘ has its correspondence in the labour pain of a birthing mother.

These fallen angels then ‚mix with the daughters of Mankind‘ (see Genesis 6) and by this they are ‚among us‘ down here, INSIDE ourselves, constantly influencing our thoughts and feelings (or at least trying to do so), tempting us whereever possible to ‚ask unnecessary questions‘, to follow the will of our lower urges seeking their short-term-oriented pseudo-pleasure in the details of the manifold world of appearance around us, instead of turning to our Creator and fulfilling our purpose of ‚bringing back home‘ that whole manifoldness of creation, by experiencing it in the context of overall unity with

106

the Source it flows from.

And in the end: It is only ‚the lot‘ that brings decision, WHICH ‚goat‘ will be the one for the Eternal One, and which is going to be brought to ‚Azazel‘; so it is ‚coincidence‘, ‚destiny‘ that makes the decision, no logical thinking, no rationality, which side (inside us) is the one ‚towards the devil‘ and which is the one leading to the Eternal. The one for the Eternal is brought to the High Priest then. The other one is taken by an ‚ish ithi‘, meaning ‚man of time‘, and brought to a cliff and thrown down from there, ’splitting into uncountable many pieces‘.

Both sides are present in every human being, even IF the ‚Azazel‘-side may be very light, and the ‚God‘-side would be very heavy, still the ‚tendency towards the devil must be there at least a little bit. It is indeed even important. Because by this tendency we get the necessary confrontation, and by confrontation we get tested and purified, like gold and silver in the refining furnace. It is this questioning of Azazel inside ourself, wanting to know and understand everything in its manifoldness, instead of the mere and ineffable experience of the unity, the oneness. And the right behaviour towards that ‚Azazel inside us‘ is the asking: ‚why DO I want to ‚know it all‘ in the split-apart manifoldness?!‘

This Azazel-tendency doesnt appear so much in a human being as something ‚perverted‘, ‚deviant‘, ‚devilish‘, as we would imagine it from Hollywood movies and stuff like that … It comes rather in a decent costume, ‚reasonably‘ asking for the purpose of things, trying to explain and make things ‚easier‘ by understanding them, making them ‚better‘ through

107

(supposedly) ‚own‘ creativity … It is a temptation to keep asking for the next answer, becoming slowly but steady more and more a heavy ‚addiction to understanding and explaining‘.

The solution in this sign is, to accept both sides of it. To choose the side of ‚unity‘, but while doing so, not to detest the other side, the side of the manifoldness. Because without the ladder (meaning also: without rationality, understanding and precise thinking) there would be only chaos in the longing for ‚unity‘, and we would never be truly reaching it. And on the other hand, the manifoldness is not to be appreciated as such alone, but only when bound together in the consciousness of unity, bringing the meaning to the manifold perspectives, to not let them diverge further and further endlessly, until no return is possible for the one losing himself into these infinite possibilities of ‚understanding‘ and ‚(re-)searching‘.

The second sign in the ‚fruit‘ group is Saggitarius; the ‚archer‘, the ‚guy with bow and arrow‘. In Hebrew this sign is called ‚qesheth‘, which just means ‚bow, arch‘. With this archetypical picture the Hebrew attempt does not so much symbolize the ‚hunter‘, but more the one 'searching and hoping for fruit‘: the arrows shot with that bow thus are seen like 'seed being cast out‘ (we may think of the greek and roman mythical figure of ‚Amor‘ or ‚Cupid‘, that ‚little baby angel‘ shooting his arrows blindly to the hearts of people, hoping for ‚fruit‘ in the sense, that the people hit by his arrows fall in love with each other and thus ‚bring fruit‘ in the very physical sense afterwards, as having children together …).

In this sign we human beings feel and are driven by a

108

very strong ‚longing for fruit'. Looking at all the contradictions of this world … we just HAVE to come to the conclusion: this cannot be the end of it! So we expect ‚fruit', somehow; we expect that, which will bring meaning to all the contradictions and disappointments of this world – whatever exactly that will be. Sagittarius just ‚won't accept' a complete meaninglessness …

The 'shooting of the arrow(s)' in this sign corresponds to the asking for the secret of this paradox world; and it is a hoping, that this questioning will bring that fruit we long for. No coincidence, that Sagittarius is exactly the NINTH of the signs (both, in the ‚circular counting' of the babylonian system watching the visible night sky, as well as in the counting through the 4 female, 3 male and 5 fruit signs in the Hebrew approach – no other sign of the Zodiac has the same ordinary number in BOTH systems, so Sagittarius in this sense is ‚the connection between the Hebrew world of Being and the Babylonian world of Becoming'): nine months it takes until the physical ‚human fruit', the baby is there. And ‚months' in the Hebrew are literally ‚renewings', since the moon is ‚renewing herself' once in this period of time.

In the more unconscious area such a ‚longing for fruit' is typically expressed as a strong desire for results of our own deeds and actions. The ‚left side' of this state of being would be a dodgy ‚perfectionism', when in the first place the (personal) 'success' is the aim of our actions and our engagements. The ‚right side' of it on the other hand is the desire and longing for fruit in a more spiritual sense, feeling directly challenged by the experience of all the already mentioned ‚contradictions of life‘, to find a form of ‚fruitful synthesis‘ of them.

But of course, there is the danger, too, that a human being in this sign does not even WANT the fruit, that he or she is indeed even fearing it, preferring instead the contradictions of life and just 'staying in them‘, and by this: staying fruitless, 'sterile‘ rather, even ‚having fun‘ with all the contradictions (maybe as a ‚cynic‘, maybe constantly self-loathing, maybe as a ‚promiscuitive‘ who is only striving for physical pleasure accompanied by an active avoiding of physical fruit, or maybe even as a convinced criminal in the most evil sense without any guilty conscience). It would be a choosing then of only the one side of life we know already, while the other side we prefer leaving out from the beginning on, we just won't ‚receive‘ this other side, even when it would be given to us as a present.

This is the ‚fear of the fruit‘; the contradictions of life are pressuring so heavily that there seems to be no possibility of a fruit developing OUT OF these contradictions. And the main contradiction in this world of course is represented in the ‚male-female‘-antagony, though not only in the physical, but of course specifically in the physical dimension, too.

What is FRUIT? It is a synthesis of the contradictions, of two opposites, of ‚the parents‘ so to speak; a synthesis that is MORE than a mere counting together. Like the child is MORE than only father plus mother – true ‚fruit‘ is uniting aspects of both of them, but still being itself something completely new. This ‚Child‘, the ‚Fruit‘ of an

110

encounter of two opposites, originates in the most intimate wish of the parents for knowing each other. By the way: in the Bible one of the commonly used euphemisms for 'sexual intercourse' is ‚to know each other'.

From purely scientific examinations of the world (no matter how ‚correctly' they are done) there will never come true fruit, only another scientific examination (this would be symbolically called ‚female homosexuality', something not explicitly ‚forbidden' in the Bible) … The same is true for only combining mystical visions with more mystical visions: only another mystical experience will come from that, but not true fruit (this would symbolically be ‚male homosexuality', which is something explicitly 'not recommended' for the People of God, see Leviticus 18,22). Only when both sides of perception of life come together, it will result in something which can be truly called ‚fruit'.

This noticeable difference of the biblical judgement concerning male and female homosexuality is to be understood from the spiritual sense: ‚male homosexuality' symbolically refers to the ‚unfruitful coming together of two entities' in the SPIRITUAL and brings forth (spiritual) ‚death' (see Leviticus 20,13), while ‚female homosexuality' refers to the ‚unfruitful coming together of two entities' in the ‚only' material world – which would be of course still something ‚fruitless' (because neither out of two men having sexual intercourse with each other, nor out of two women having sexual intercourse with each other there will ever come a baby), but it would be nothing ‚causing spiritual death', as long as it

111

remains to be practiced only in this 'superficial', material world.

So in this understanding, biblically there is NO actual ,prohibition' of physical (= ,female') homosexuality for human beings (of whatever 'sex' in their appearing side of being) in this world; only the 'spiritual' (= ,male') form of homosexuality we are seriously warned of, because it necessarily leads to (spiritual) ,death' for the entities taking part in it.

Coming back to the characteristics of the sign of Sagittarius again: The human being in this sign ALREADY owns this fruit as a hidden potential inside him/herself; and it would be a pity if he/she won't bring it forth in this life. It is like human beings, which in general have the potency of physical regenerativity, of having children. But they nonetheless have the possibility, too, to reject this potential, to have no children; be it, because they prefer ,only having fun', only strive for their own lust, or be it out of any other reason. From the point of view of the Eternal this would be a pity of course.

With true fruit in the spiritual sense, it is like in the New Testament with the ,Son of God', the Messiah, who does not come out of a purely ,biological' conception, where only ,the horizontal multiplies with itself'. He rather comes from ,the vertical impact into this horizontal world' (,the Virgin impregnated by the Spirit of Holyness'), and so He can never be truly understood if only looked at from the ,biological', physical and material, historical point of view. He is ,Eternity incarnated into history', but by this, He is NEVER reduceable to this one human existence in history of so-called ,Jesus of

112

Nazareth'. He is Eternal, He was before and He will be afterwards as ‚Son of Man', ‚Son of God', as ‚Messiah'.

And such is the true ‚Salvation': although it is experienced in this world as something being ‚achieved' or ‚being granted' at a specific point in life, in time, it nevertheless is known then to have already been there before, only not recognized yet. And by this insight there is no more fear to ‚lose it' again, because even IF you would lose it (seemingly) in this life again, you would be sure that it still IS there, no matter if you keep experiencing it directly or not.

In the same way, ‚fruit' is something, once experienced, never disappearing again for good. Because what shows up in this world as a representative of the Eternal, is understood as actually being from another world, only being present HERE, too, now. And this is the great difference to the ‚male' signs: the fruit signs are fully accomplished INSIDE this world of the female, horizontal principle, making the hidden, male, abstract ‚Heavenly Father' and his Messages (and Messengers) visible as ‚the Son(s) and Daughter(s)', as the Children of God here down on Earth, or rather: down here, being born OUT OF Earth.

Mankind in the sign of Sagittarius is characterized by this desire and deep longing for this ‚coming together of horizontal and vertical reality' as something experienceable in THIS world, as ‚the fruit'.

The third (and by this, the ‚central') of the five signs in the ‚fruit group' of the Zodiac is Gemini, the

Twins; in Hebrew ‚theomim‘ (= ‚twins‘, too). Being the third in a row, as it is typical, in this sign again the strong duality is the essential of it. The third generation of the Patriarchs of the People of Israel, the generation after Abraham and his son Isaac, namely Isaacs two sons, are twins: Jacob and Esau; the ‚Appearing One‘ and the ‚Hidden One‘, how they are symbolically interpreted in the tradition.

It is emphatically recommended in the Ancient Wisdom: the ‚Appearing One‘, too, shall be accepted as he is. He is not to be detested for being supposedly ‚unspiritual‘ or something like that. And on the other side: ‚the Secret‘, the Hidden One, shall not be forced into appearance, because that would take the sense away from him, from ‚it‘.

The mythical ‚Jacob‘ is identical to everything in a human being, which is there inside, but cannot come into visibility, which cannot be pronounced, articulated (for whatever individual reason!). We know, we WOULD articulate it, if we would be able to do so – but we just can't.

And every try to reveal the hidden secret, would be a desecrating, and thus it is recommended to never even try to; in any way this revealing of the innermost secret is to be avoided. When it SHALL be revealed, it will reveal itself, surprisingly. It needs to be waited in patience for that moment.

The mythical picture of the ‚battle‘ between ‚Appearing One‘ and ‚Hidden One‘ is biblically experienced in the story of Jacob and Esau. And we know from the story of the Bible (see Genesis 25,21ff), who is going to be the winner: Jacob. But it

114

is a heavenly decision, nothing that would be ‚just‘, a matter of understandable ‚justice‘, from the human point of view. For Esau actually it is quite tragic, because he does not know why he is losing.

And we all know this situation: we all tend to have things in the world of the appearing, which we strive for – but then we never achieve them. We dream, we wish for it … but we see soon: it shall not be. Be it a love, a friendship, a certain career, or any form of success; much of it will always remain a mere dream. Life stays ‚cold‘ concerning our hopes, it just ‚goes on‘, without granting us the ‚great miracle‘ we hoped for. And with time we get accustomed to that, we are satisfied more or less with the little we get. We know: others have an even worse fate to bear than we have. So why complaining …

With the experience of this mythical story of Jacob and Esau the question arises in ourselves: why, to what purpose is all the suffering? Why am I appearing here in this world – and death in the end is a sure thing for me?! … at least that is how it looks like.

And that's why ‚Esau weeps‘ (see Genesis 27,38). He is the first figure in the Bible of whom it is told explicitly that he weeps. Because he sees: The blessing, seemingly destined for ME, is granted to the other one.

And we, too, think: In this life here, in this world, HERE it should be, here we have all the people we love, the people we like, here we will achieve everything that would be worth keeping for ever. But then everything seems to be quite different, ‚the other one' already was here, has taken ‚our part' of the blessing; we are ‚too late'.

The weeping occurs exactly when Esau realizes, that his father Isaac has ‚blessed the wrong son', his brother Jacob, and Isaac explains: I thought I would have blessed you, I really thought that it is going to be YOU, the Appearing One, who will be blessed here in the appearing side of life! But someone else came here instead of you, deceiving me, taking that blessing. I don't even know how that happened!

In the Bible one name for God is ‚the Terror, the Startling of Isaac', in Hebrew ‚Pachad Yitzchak'; and in the tradition it is explained: it is actually THIS exact terror Isaac felt, when he realized, how his blessing has not reached the ‚right son' from his point of view, that it has not reached Esau, the one ‚whom he loved (more)' (see Genesis 25,28).

So the ‚Terror of Isaac' also is the insight, the sudden realization, that God's ways are sometimes so shockingly different than any human would think of them (see Isaiah 55,8: ‚my thoughts are not your thoughts, my ways are not your ways, saith the Lord'). There is this ‚other, secret side' of things, we do not see, but which is so heavily important that it can be really startling to us, terrorizing even, to become aware of this heavy importance; and never really be able to understand it (yes, we always want to ‚understand' everything, it's the Azazel-side in us …).

The human being in the sign of the Twins, of Gemini, could have developed a high consciousness of this question for the reason and purpose of the suffering

116

in this sense, this great conflict of the appearing and the hidden side of life, and of the startling felt, when we realize HOW great that conflict is and how painful for the appearing side of us it can get. (A similar conflict, only from a little different perspective, will be looked at in the next part, when describing the characteristics of the planet Mars. And by the way, like Mars is considered the direct opposite to Venus in the overall harmony of the 7 planets, the sign of Gemini is in direct opposition to the sign of Virgo in the visible circle of the Zodiac on the night sky above us; and Virgo in a similar way is associated to Venus, as Gemini is to Mars.)

But there always is the ‚Jacob'-side, too. Jacob comes with Esau together into this world by ‚holding the heel' of Esau, so he ‚tricks himself in', so to speak (we already looked at the different possible translations of the name of Jacob in the last part).

So on this way the invisible comes into our life: by holding fast, attaching itself to the visible (and probably kind of ‚against the will' of the visible itself …). And this invisible is going ‚to win' in the end. But what does this victory of the invisible mean?

In the New Testament there is talked much about the ‚Kingdom coming' (referring to the ‚Kingdom of God, of Heaven'), and always it is clear: this kingdom WILL be here, IN this world, too, in the end. But it does not come FROM this world, it originates ‚on the other side', comes as something invisible, and we are even warned to not ‚expect it as coming from this world' and not as ‚coming in a way like the way would be, on which anything from this world would be coming'. It WILL reach this world,

117

yes … but first there is the suffering, the betrayal, denial, torture, even the crucifixion. Afterwards is the resurrection.

But why do we have to go through all the evil before? Why can't it be directly only the ,Good' for us here in this world? The final answer is only given in the sign of Leo. But in Gemini this question in the best case begins to ,bring fruit' already, by raising the right further questions to be asked.

Jacobs mythical confrontation with Esau is happening for us in every moment of life anew. We always have this fight, this struggle inside us: the fight over the decision to which of the two sides we are tending in this or that situation. Are we more preferring the appearing side, like it would be ,what the world expects us to do'? Or do we dare to turn to the mysterious, to the hidden instead, not being understood by most of our surrounding world? And at some point there IS indeed the certainty, that the true blessing is in the invisible, in the mysterious, the ineffable, in the hidden – in that which is even deliberately hiding ITSELF.

We should look a little bit deeper into the concept of ,blessing' in the Hebrew understanding, since the two unequal twin brothers are having their life-long battle especially for the ,blessing' of their father. The Hebrew word for ,blessing' is ,barakh', written with the three letters B-R-Kh. So the word has a numeric structure of 2-200-20 and a numeric value of 222; thus it can be identified as something ,affecting the world of duality on every level'. On this background, in the tradition a true ,blessing' is defined as something being ,unlimitedly realized on the

118

physical level of existence, too'. So ,being blessed' with anything, cannot mean to only ,have' or ,enjoy' something in the inward experience of life, but the blessing has to be present reaching deep into the ,hard physical' existence, too, into ,the world of the (number) 2'.

Jacob is fleeing, because Esau wants to kill him now, for 'stealing his blessing'. So this only 'surreptitiously obtained' blessing, in the first place for Jacob becomes something, which is forcing him out of the world of his brother, out of the world of the appearing. 22 years he is gone (again we have this ,Two' on every level here), in this ,time' (or stage) the Appearing One is getting strong, Esau is becoming wealthy and mighty. But Jacob himself, although in a far away country (the country of his mother's origin), is also growing; in his possession AND in his experience. In the 22 years of service for his uncle ,Laban' (a name meaning ,whitening'; ,becoming light') Jacob gets tricked himself by Laban, so he has to experience his own trickiness as ,the one on the other side' now. But with God's Help he still gains wealth and marries his two wives (the daughters of his uncle) and his two concubines in these years of hard work.

Those mythical '22 years' are thus for us today, too, a ,getting strong of the secret, of the mystery' in the hidden background (in that ,far away country'), while in our appearing side of life (in ,Esau's country') we may seem to be only looking for the appearing, having forgotten about all the hidden things we were curious about when we still were innocent, 'naive' children. ,Esau', the ,outwardly

119

oriented' in us is even hating his brother ‚Jacob', the 'secret', still wanting to kill him, kill ‚it'.

And then, after the 22 years, ‚Jacob returns to his homeland', to finally dare the crucial confrontation with Esau.

Coming into the land of his brother, the messengers he sent forth to Esau to appease him with gifts, come back to Jacob announcing: ‚Your brother approaches you with 400 men' (and they are more or less implying by this: ‚and he wants to crush you!' …).

What now occurs, is the famous 'struggle of Jacob with an angel at the river Jabbok' (Genesis 32,24-32): after bringing his whole family and his stuff over the river, he goes back alone one last time – and suddenly ‚a man wrestles with him, until the breaking of the day'. Jacob fights, but neither he nor ‚the man' can win; and at daybreak ‚the man' begs Jacob to let him go. Jacob is willing to do so only on the condition ‚to get blessed' by ‚the man'. And so it happens.

This enigmatic tale of Jacob fighting a strange ‚man' at the Jabbok river is a relatively short text in the Bible, but it is extensively elaborated on in the oral tradition. A wide consens has been established that the episode is describing a fight in the ‚heavenly realm', which nevertheless has its direct effect here in the world of matter, too: Esau namely cannot do anything anymore, after his ‚lord' (as whom that ‚man', some kind of angelic being, is seen) has lost (resp. NOT won) the fight with Jacob at the Jabbok river.

This river can be seen as the ‚borderline between

visible and invisible'; and Jacob thus is coming ‚from the invisible realm', going for ‚the side of the visible', ‚Esau's side', where he wants to ‚have his place, too' now – that is the actual meaning of the ‚blessing' Jacob is asking from the angel.

In the tradition there is a stress on a (supposed) ‚fact' which is said to be the reason for Jacob staying behind all the rest of his family alone at the river part: he forgot ‚a little broken cup' of his stuff on the other side of the river, where they had their last resting place. And although this broken little thing has no actual material ‚value', Jacob values it as a part of his belongings nevertheless, and thus goes back to take it. By this he shows to the Heavens that he looks ‚for the quality, and not (only) for quantity', that he bases his actions not solely on the question ‚what purpose, what benefit' they serve, but tries to do just what is right in his understanding. And only because of this manner of looking at the things, Jacob is there at the river part in the crucial moment and gets the chance for this fight, resulting in the blessing he always hoped for.

This story of someone, who is taking a risk (or ‚a great toil') on himself, only for a seemingly ‚minor, worthless thing' to save, is usually compared to another story of the oral tradition: The story of Moses and how he got to the famous ‚burning bush', where he has his first encounter with the Eternal One calling him to redeem His People out of Egypt (Exodus 3,1ff). In this tale Moses is still a shepherd with his sheep, and one day one little lamb is lost. It would have been not much loss in the material sense, enough sheep are going to birth new lambs soon, so

121

that one lamb lost would be no ‚rational reason‘ to leave the whole flock alone to search after the one little lost one. But, as ‚the good shepherd‘, Moses goes to look for the lost lamb. And he is having a very difficult wandering ‚over stones, sticks and rocks‘, until he finally finds the poor little lamb; and in this moment he becomes aware of that burning bush, which he never would have passed on his 'normal' way with the whole flock, if he had not searched for that little lamb in this inhospitable area.

Like a 'natural law', at this point in our journey of life – when we begin to dare to take the personal risk of ‚wasting our energy‘ only to achieve something, of what we know it is the right thing, but which would be nothing 'necessary' from a ‚worldly‘ point of view, maybe even something ‚crazy‘ from this worldly look on it; but we nonetheless decide to go for it – then we are confronted with ‚the man‘, with that angel, which could be called the ‚Angel of the Appearing‘, being the ‚lord‘ of Esau, like a ‚guardian angel‘ of the ‚Appearing One‘. This Angel of the Appearing wants to hinder the ‚Jacob‘ in ourselves, the hidden, the secret, to enter ‚his‘ world of Appearance. But Jacob ‚wins‘, he gets the blessing, the right to have a place, have space in THIS world, too.

Jacob at this point of the story gets his 'new name', ‚Israel‘, representing a renewed essence, a new character. And the name ‚Israel‘ can be translated as ‚you have (already) fought with divine and human beings and you have stood your ground‘.

The secret, the individual mystery of every single human being, has its battle, its confrontation on

122

another level of existence. And because it happens THERE, Jacob can stand his ground in front of Esau in THIS world, too, later. Esau's ‚400 men' just ‚flow away'. It is explained in the tradition, why Esau does not even TRY to fight Jacob when they finally meet: ‚like time flows away in this world of time, all his fighters have vanished one after another, until the point when Jacob finally stands in front of him (by the way, Jacob approaches Esau in 5 divisions, the number of the ‚fruit', being himself the ‚One before the four groups' of his children with their four mothers, remember the 1-4-principle ...; see Genesis 33,1-3).

In the Gemini-layer this ‚victory of Jacob' is ‚built in' already, if you will. He fights his battles ‚on another side', that's why ‚down here' he has it easy. Only, if he does NOT fight his battles on the other side, it is very difficult here for him. Jacob can only 'stand his ground' here, if he arrives here consciously ‚from thereof'. And ‚from thereof' means for our individual approach to life: ‚always think of the QUALITY of the things!'; don't look only for the purpose to yourself, for your own benefit, when you do something! Then you are ‚going back over the Jabbok for the ‚one little broken cup', and you will have that fight with the ‚Angel of Appearance', granting you the blessing in the end.

Maybe you think in some moments of life: I always wanted the best, but I earn only bad, even evil reactions. Nevermind! You fought and won ON THE OTHER SIDE. That's enough, you WILL be blessed here, in the end at least. Trust.

Then ‚the kingdom manifests itself in your life'. The

123

mystery then ‚has become flesh'. That is the secret of ‚blessing', of truly ‚being blessed' in the actual biblical sense of this expression.

The fourth zodiacal sign of the ‚fruit group' (and also the fourth sign in the babylonian mode of counting the 12 along their circle on the night sky) is Cancer, or in Hebrew 'sartan', which both means ‚crab' or ‚crayfish'. This sign is either ‚the 11th of the 12 signs' in the Hebrew order of discussing them, or it is ‚the 9th of the 10', when we take the three male signs as the unity they actually are. And in this mode of counting, as ‚the ninth', Cancer is especially representing the ‚9th day of creation', which we already touched on in the last part. As this ‚9th day' it is associated with the ‚journey through the underworld', after which the final 10th day gets born out of this ‚underworld', as the reaching of the Oneness of our origin, but now ‚on the next level'.

This ‚ten' symbolizes the ‚collective salvation', like the ‚eight' symbolizes the ‚individual' one. After having 'sacrificed again' the ladder ‚individual salvation' of the ‚eight', and by this, having deliberately taken that ‚journey through the underworld' of the 'nine', the individual salvation ‚ressurrects' as the potential of ‚becoming a living symbol of salvation yourself for the benefit of your surrounding world' in the ‚ten'.

This ‚journey through the underworld' can be experienced in this sign of Cancer – in both of its dimensions: as the suffering path through a hostile realm (like probably most people would understand the term ‚journey through the underworld' …); and

124

also as the realization of this ‚underworld' being a ‚womb' indeed, out of which the Divine ‚Child' will be born into the ‚New (perception of the) World'.

So, Cancer is the 4th fruit sign and the 4th sign in the visible circle of the Zodiac. We already established the importance of the number 4, especially in this ‚world of the 4' we live in as physical beings, this ‚female world' of ‚duality in its fulfillment' (see again the very first part of this introduction). For the sign of Cancer we will now meditate on a certain aspect of this 'number 4' in the context of our world of the seven days, by looking at the fourth ‚word of God' in the creation week of Genesis chapter 1 (Genesis 1,11).

As always at ‚a third in a row' a ‚twin' appears, on the third day of creation week, too, there is not only one ‚word of God', but there are TWO words of God; the second word of God on that third day thus is the fourth word of God in total. This fourth word of God is concerning the creation of plant life on the dry area of the Earth, which is commonly translated as ‚grass, herbs and trees bearing fruit'. And in the second account of the creation-story (second chapter of Genesis) it is also the fourth deed of God (after creating ‚mist', ‚man' and a ‚garden/guarded realm'), which is concerning the plants: it is the growth of ‚every tree that is pleasant to the sight and good for food', and especially ‚the two trees' in the midst of the ‚Garden' (Genesis 2,9) …

These (in-)famous ‚two trees' then are the crucial factor determining the further progress of the story: the ‚Tree of Life' versus the other tree, the one of ‚knowledge of Good and Evil', of which it is said to

125

Mankind: ‚you shall not eat of it, for in the day you eat thereof, you shall die the death‘ (Genesis 2,17). These two trees could also be named the ‚tree of being‘ (= Tree of Life) and the ‚tree of becoming‘ (= Tree of Knowledge of Good and Evil).

Here we see the connection to the first account of the story, where the word was of a ‚tree that is fruit and makes fruit‘ (if we translate the verse of Genesis 1,11 more literally), but then only a ‚tree that makes fruit‘ is appearing (Genesis 1,12). The obvious contradiction for our world of duality, to let appear a ‚tree that already IS fruit, as well as it is still MAKING fruit, that means: bringing forth fruit‘ – this contradiction is 'solved‘ by the Earth by … just ‚ignoring it‘ … Earth is withstanding the will of God: the ‚unambiguous‘ comes instead, only the ‚Becoming‘ (of fruit on the tree) will be possible in this world of time and space, not the ‚already-Being (fruit in itself) AND at the same time a still-Becoming (developing towards fruit)‘.

On the fourth day, with the fifth deed of creation, it is the same on another level: two great lights shall appear, but only one big and one little appear. And the little one, the Moon, is even being kind of 'strange‘, rhythmically increasing and decreasing in size and changing in shape, sometimes being on the day visible, not only in the night, where she ‚belongs‘. The Sun in the contrary is that, what 'stays the same all the time‘.

So again we see in these ‚two lights on the sky‘ the ‚one of becoming‘ (Moon), and the ‚one of being‘ (Sun), but separated, one for the day, the other for the night. But ‚the one for the night‘, the ‚becoming

126

one', is sometimes present in day-time, too, somehow. So in eternity, ,in the Being', there IS time, there IS development, there IS becoming, too (we already touched this matter when mentioning the one possible translation of the Hebrew word for ,Heaven', being ,there is water').

It is said: in the layer of Cancer in every human being there is this experience of BOTH: ,being' AND ,becoming' in One.

But when we hear statements like this, we say: Well, then where is he, that old man over there, as still being a young man?! He is old now, as we clearly can see, but I know, he used to be much younger back then, he looked totally different ... if indeed ,both is in One, being and becoming', then: WHERE is that young man of the past time gone now?

We get an idea, that the true eternity must have all the stages of the life of this man ,at one sight' somehow, and not even only the stages of his fleshly life in the body, but the states before his conception and after his death, too. A vision, not really graspable for our limited capacity of understanding as human beings in this ,world of the 4'.

But this secret of the possibility of a so-called ,coincidentia oppositorum', that is: of a ,falling together of the opposites', is also present in the ,ineffable' name of God in the Bible, which is typically translated as ,Lord', but actually more precisely as ,Eternal One': that famous Hebrew word built up of the four letters Yod-Heh-Waw-Heh, ,YHWH', sometimes pronounced ,Jahweh' or ,Jehowah' or ,Jahwah'. But actually it is just NOT

127

pronouncable at all in ONE definite ‚correct' version, because its heavy and unmeasureable meaning lies especially in the variety of possible translations. But ‚grammatically' interpreted it is the Hebrew word for ‚being, existing; happening, occuring' in the masculine singular, but in an ambiguous form, meaning ‚he is existing', as well as ‚he will exist' and ‚he has been existing', at the same time.

Another famous name of God is found in the scripture with Moses and the ‚burning bush' (Exodus 3,1ff). Here (answering the question of Moses, what he should say to the Israelites who that God is that is promising to liberate them out of Egypt) the Eternal One defines Himself with the following words: ‚I am who I am'; but it can be equally translated as ‚I will be who I will be'. Or even as something like ‚I will be happening, as what (ever) I will be happening'.

Seeing only the ‚becoming' means seeing death, and not only a physical, bodily death, but the disappearing of every single moment, of every experience in life. That is the form of ‚death' we constantly are experiencing in this world of becoming.

‚Being' is ETERNAL and infinite, so it contains also the ‚Becoming' in itself already. But we are focused on the ‚becoming-half of it' only, because we have ‚chosen to eat of the wrong tree in the Garden', of that one which ‚makes fruit' (but IS not already fruit) …

The Cancer-layer inside us has a very good feeling of the true essence of Being, has the chance to reach out for the ‚Tree of Life'. This tree is still always present

128

in yourself in this layer of your being. As it is said: ,the Tree of Life is available for those who reach for it'. But the other tree, the one of ,knowledge of good and evil', is much more present IN THIS WORLD, it can be seen, calculated, sensed and … ,is logical', ,lawful'. The Tree of Life is not. The Tree of Life is ,crazy', so to speak, not of this world, 'not fitting in', for most people here.

That is exactly what makes THIS world a form of the ,underworld'. And ,underworld' is the word ,She'ol' in Hebrew, a word literally meaning ,the questioning' or ,the demanding', and this can refer to a ,torturing asking, without any answers ever given', as well as to the ,demanding force of death, not letting a single soul go through this world of time and space without dying once'.

But already INSIDE this ,underworld' we live in, we have indeed the Eternal present, too; we only have to reach out for it, BELIEVING that it is here for us, as ,being the fruit ALREADY', not only as ,bringing fruit' afterwards.

Let's put it this way, being a little bit provocative: You only are afraid of death, because you do not believe in the resurection as ,an already happened fact' (although for yourself only paradoxically ,happened in the future', when looking at it from our timely perspective …). Are you also afraid of going to bed in the night? Fearing to not wake up in the morning? Although you have already seen other people standing up again after sleeping … It is the SAME with physical death, only on another level.

And yes of course: the human being in Cancer HAS

the other side, too, the tendency for the ‚causal‘, rational understanding and judging. He CAN feel lost in the ‚underworld‘, be it seeing this world here already as that underworld, or fearing to come there afterwards, as into the ‚valley of death‘, where the passed away souls go, the ‚Hades‘ of greek mythology.

But, compared to all the other signs of the Zodiac, this Cancer-layer in all of us is indeed especially shaped by the experience of the Tree of Life inside him- or herself. This experience is his or her ‚trump‘.

A human being in the sign of Cancer can easily 'show fruit‘ here, in this world, representing the other side already in here. By that, this ‚underworld‘ becomes a ‚womb‘, a matrix, in which ‚the fruit ripes‘, before it is born on the coming day, on the 10th. The Hebrew letter with the numeric value 9, Teth, is consequently associated with the ‚womb‘, as well as with ‚potter's clay‘, the raw material out of which the ‚creator‘ makes his new creations. Because here, in the ninth day (as which our ‚world of the four‘ will be experienced from a certain point on – at the latest when we have physically died), in this ‚underworld‘, in the ‚demanding and asking‘ sphere of death – here it is developing, what then becomes born into the ‚World to Come‘ of the ‚tenth day‘.

Leo (the 5th in the circle of the 12 signs on the night sky), the ‚lion‘, is the fifth and last of the zodiacal signs in the ‚fruit group‘. Its Hebrew name is ‚aryeh‘, which equally means ‚lion‘; but the 4 consonant letters of this word, Aleph-Resh-Yod-Heh, are also readable as ‚or yah‘, which is translateable then as

130

‚Light of the Eternal One'. This very last sign in the Hebrew order of discussion of the 12 signs is the one which is most thoroughly associated with ‚the Messiah', as the end and aim of All. After the ‚four' of the 4 first fruit signs, Leo is ‚the One' of the 1-4-principle, finally fulfilling the purpose of this ‚world of the four' by transcending it, without leaving or annihilating it, but by reigning over it, ruling in it, as the true and eternal ‚King of the Universe' (one of the many names of God, in Hebrew ‚Melekh ha Olam').

One reason, why exactly Leo is viewed as THE very Messianic sign, is that the Lion is traditionally seen as a symbol for the tribe of Judah, of which the Messiah originates in His incarnation as a human being, be it in the christian sense as the Christ Jesus, or be it in the jewish understanding of the Mashiach as the One still awaited to come as the ‚Ben Dawid'. But whatever stance one takes on this question, in any case this belonging of the Messiah to the tribe of Judah is to be understood ‚mythically', too, not only in the ‚genetical sense' of being literally born into the ethnic group of ‚the Jews'. For the name ‚Judah', actually more correctly transliterated and pronounced as ‚Yehudah', means literally ‚praise of God', ‚praise of the Eternal', and thus refers to the character of the incarnated Messiah as a human being appearing in perfect resemblance of our Creator, representing Him in any regard and by this, honoring Him to the fullest, and making all the people around Himself to become aware of Him and ‚praise the Eternal' for being granted to experience the presence of His Messiah in all His Glory.

In the Leo-layer of your being you can be knowing that YOU ARE KING already (just for the fact that you are a human being, created in the resemblance of the Eternal, to rule as a spiritual being over the matter inside this world). You are ,born as a king', you do not have to ,achieve it' first through any deeds, or by learning to be one.

And being a true king means: reigning over the WHOLE kingdom, not only over parts of it. This mythical picture contains the fact that in a real kingdom on Earth there always are healthy people in your land, as well as sick people, rich people. as well as poor people, good people, as well as evil ones. The true king reigns and rules over ALL of them, ,from one end of the kingdom to the other end of it'. And this mythical picture transported into a personal existence as a ,Royal Servant of the Eternal One' inside this world of time and space also means: the Messiah Jesus has to perish physically, has to suffer and to be defeated first in this world, before he can resurrect and bring the Kingdom of the Heavens into THIS world, too. He achieves it, by having ,penetrated all life', and for this world of duality we live in with our bodies, this ,penetrating of all life' contains to even penetrate, experience DEATH during our journey down here.

The ,Kingdom of God' here in this world always comes as a 'sudden breakthrough' from out of another realm. But it does not come by force, not by the power of anyone inside this world who is trying to bring it here. If you want to achieve it with strenght and power and force, you will perish like Samson perishes in the biblical story of the last of the 'judges' of Israel, before they get their first king (see Judges chapters 13-16): Samson (actually more correctly pronounced as 'Shimshon', from the word 'shemesh', meaning 'sun') is famous for his superhuman bodily strenght, and for using it to kill a lion with his bare hands, and for often fighting alone against many enemies at once. But he is IN-famous, too, for killing himself in the end in a sort of 'suicide attack', killing 'more enemies in his death than he killed in his whole life'.

Beside this, Samson is married to a woman called 'Deleylah', symbolizing the 'night' (in Hebrew 'leylah'), which eventually seduces him to tell her his 'secret of power' (which turns out to be his long hair, which then is cut off by his enemies to defeat him). And so Samson gets into captivity and slavery, until his hair has grown back his old lenght, so that he can free himself with his recovered superhuman strenght again.

In the oral tradition concerning this scriptural account of Samson it is told: Samson perishes, because he tries to be a redeemer 'out of his own power'. Yes, he is 'mighty as the Sun' with his great strenght, with his long hair resembling a lion's mane or the shining rays of the sun – but what he lacks is the aspect of being a humble servant despite his great power. Like the sun on the sky is only following his pathway as it is determined by the Eternal, not abusing his power to follow 'own ways'. Not-so-coincidentally, in Hebrew the word for 'sun' means 'servant', too.

This kind of 'Service' will be the actual duty of the true 'King' inside you: Using the strenght and power granted to you by the grace of the Eternal One only

133

for the spread of His glory, by performing the divine love for all your fellow human beings around you in this world.

Now, on the end of this fourth part, it shall be looked once again at the symbolism of the '10 days' in some more detail. And this we will do by drawing the parallels between the signs of the Zodiac (in their ‚visible' order in their circular shape of the night sky) and the 7 days of creation week plus the additional ‚3 days' representing the ‚3 stages of salvation' fulfilling this world of the seven days, how the Ancient Wisdom describes them. We will thus see a correspondence of the signs and these ‚days'.

Taurus represents, as we have seen in the second part of this introduction, a ‚breakthrough from another reality'. And by this it is corresponding to the first day of creation week, where All, the complex of ‚Heavens and Earth', just appears ‚out of nothing', like as already having been there before somehow (‚in the imagination of God'). But there is still ‚raw force' predominating on the surface of creation (‚the Earth was without form and void, and darkness upon the face of the depth', see verse 2); like the ‚bull power' is such a raw force even today in every human beings ‚layer of Taurus'. So the creation gets its first proportioning (the ‚light', and then the separation between light and darkness) just by the call of God.

In Aries we are confronted with a fact, which actually already originates in the very beginning (1st verse of the Bible): the duality of ‚Heavens and Earth', which was created already kind of ‚before' the first day, before the first ‚word' of God, so ‚in silence', like the

134

Lamb is famous for his silence. But only now on this 2nd day this duality comes to the visible, as the ‚firmament', called ‚heaven', dividing the ‚waters above and below' (verses 6-8).

In the sign of Pisces we saw that there is a specific dual nature, which is depicted in the ‚two fish' symbol of this sign, too: on one side the fish as ‚feeling good inside the water', inside its element of life; and on another side the fish ‚longing for being fished out of the waters', out of this world of time and space. So on this third day of creation we see the development of the two sides of ‚earthly reality': the area of the ‚waters down here' (= of time and space world) and that of the ‚dry land' (the eternal realm of myth and dream inside us, we experience during our earthly life parallel to the time-space-realm around us); so by this the necessary fundament (water to swim, dry land to be fished out) for the later appearance of ‚the actual fish' is established on this day (because as an actual animal that fish is yet to come, on the fifth day, because, as representing the 'souls of mankind', the fish has to ‚come out of the vertical dimension of reality', out of ‚the male signs' of the 5th day, while the first four days still represent only the horizontal dimension, the ‚female signs'). Beside this, on this third day (as every third with that ‚twin-nature' …) in its second half there is the beginning of actual life in this physical world: the plants grow out of the dry land (so symbolically: the first fundament for any later and ‚higher' forms of life grows ‚out of the eternal sphere').

As characterizing Aquarius we established the idea of ‚handling, reigning over' the ‚times' (symbolized by the ‚waters‘ the bucket of the water carrier scoops, carries and pours out according to his will). And on this fourth day, too, the ‚times‘, especially night and day, are being ‚reigned‘ and ‚ruled‘ by means of the ‚great lights on the firmament of the material sky‘.

The fifth day of creation now is characterized by the first impact of the ‚vertical‘, and can be seen as represented by the unity of the three ‚male signs‘ Virgo+Libra+Scorpio. In the development of creation we here look at the beginning of the actual ‚movement‘ in a ‚vertical‘ dimension; the first ‚moving life‘ (after the only stationary plant life of day three) is coming into play: birds and fish going ‚towards the upper and lower waters‘, the birds flying towards the ‚firmament‘ (which seperates the ‚upper waters‘ from the earthly realm, as seen on day two), and the fish swimming in the ‚lower waters‘ down here. Maybe in these two animal forms we can see a materialized symbol of our own dual nature of the ‚two souls‘, spoken about in the first part of this introduction: the ‚fish‘ being the ‚animalistic soul‘ (nephesh), and the ‚birds‘ being the ‚divine soul‘ (neshamah) – one being bound to this world of waters, of time; the other being in much closer contact to the heavenly realms.

The sign of Capricorn (the first of the row of the ‚fruit signs‘) would then correspond to the sixth day (as ‚the second third‘ again a day of very ‚dual nature‘, with two major God-actions/words in it, see Genesis 1,24-31): first the creation of the ‚animal'(-istic) life on the dry land, and in the second half the creation of Mankind ‚in the resemblance of God‘, being ‚male and female‘ in one (see verse 27 in a literal translation). So it is established on this day the harmonic complementarity of ‚the manifoldness of animal life' versus ‚the oneness of Mankind', representing the ‚two goats', both necessary: one being a qurban for the Eternal One, the other being sent into the 'splitting apart' of all material creation.

In the sign of Sagittarius we then can see ‚our' seventh day, our world of time and space, as the ‚resting of God' after he has made everything and saw that ‚it was very good'; so this 7th day from God's perspective is indeed to be grasped as a ‚waiting for the outcome' of the six days, as the ‚hoping for fruit', or rather a not even doubting ‚expecting of fruit' out of the done work.

With Gemini we finally experience ‚the fight of the twins', the central fruit sign, which is resulting in the realization of ‚the 8th day' down here, as the ‚blessing of the Appearing One being granted to the invisible, mysterious side of life', or mythically speaking: ‚Jacob stealing the blessing of his brother Esau by deceiving their father with the help of their mother' (see Genesis 27,5-17).

But after (seemingly) achieving this blessing on this ‚tricky way', there nevertheless is the crucial 'split of the kingdom' again (see the third part of this introduction, the paragraph concerning the sign of Scorpio and especially therein the comments on the biblical account of the 'split of the Solomonian kingdom after Solomons death'): Jacob has to flee his homeland for 22 years, working for his deceitful uncle Laban, where Jacob will have his ‚Cancer-experience' of being ‚in the underworld', but this

137

underworld ‚being a womb‘, where his future ripes (= he marries and has his children, who will become the forefathers of the 12 tribes of Israel).

The ’ninth day‘ would then be corresponding to the sign of Cancer: We experience ‚the whole of Creation‘, or rather ‚the original wholeness of our inner and our outer perception of reality‘, as that ‚kingdom being split apart‘; and also our possibilities of ‚handling this world‘ seem to be split apart – mythically split apart into ‚the Two Trees of the Garden‘ (which actually have ONE common root, how it is explained in the tradition, and only have been ‚cut apart‘ by Mankind, making them to two distinct ‚things‘, that means: separating ‚Being‘ from ‚Becoming‘ in our perception of reality). Only by this ’split‘ the world around us becomes the so-called ‚underworld‘ threatening us with death (in Hebrew ‚She’ol‘), that means: the ‚ruthlessly demanding‘ and the ‚tortureous question-raising‘.

But finally … exactly the journey through this apparent ‚underworld‘ will result in the finding of the Tree of Life in this underworld: ultimately passing the so-called ‚Kherubim‘, those ‚watchmen‘-angels of the beginning, standing guard on the pathway towards the Tree of Life, bearing the ‚flame of the sword of (death-)revolvement‘ (see Genesis 3,24, though mostly distortedly translated as something like ‚the blade of a sword shaken‘).

As the last sign of the 12 in the Hebrew order of discussion we looked at Leo; thus Leo is representing the ’10th day‘, when ultimate salvation can be experienced, not only ‚inside oneself‘, as the one individual experiencing it, but as the whole of

138

Creation finally reaching the state of salvation. It is for the individual in this sign the final ‚achievement‘ of (or actually rather the final ‚insight into the everlasting presence of an already achieved‘) ‚kingship‘ in your own life, ‚kingship‘ of your own person. It is the coming of the Kingdom of Heavens INTO this world, as the greatest fruit a human being can bring under the best circumstances during his physical life: being a living testimony for the grace of the Eternal upon His servants, resembling His Messiah by ‚having this Messiah alive inside yourself‘, having Him AS (that also means: INSTEAD of) your (old) own being. HE is that ‚King‘ inside you, who always has been there – He only has to be recognized as who He is.

And just to make it sure: the word ‚kingship‘ here is not meant to be ‚anti-feminist‘ in any regard, but the ‚male‘ word for this final state of mastery is stressing the ‚inner‘, the spiritual character of the kingship. And the ‚Queen‘ this King is married to is: ‚the whole world‘, which is His Kingdom – and for HER that ‚King inside you‘ has to be ‚a good husband‘ in this sign of Leo!

But the whole topic of ‚the 9th and the 10th day‘, which are following after the 8th day of the ‚individual‘ salvation, will need some more depth to be understood in their vital importance. When looking at the planets, and especially at the so-called ‚hidden planets‘ in the following two parts, this more depth will hopefully be achieved.

139

The Seven visible Planets moving through the Circle of the Zodiac

The crucial difference between planets and zodiacal signs is: the planets move, while the zodiacal signs are steady. And it is especially this combination of steadiness of signs and dynamic of planets which brings the decisive unique character of every single star constellation, because this combination guarantees that never the exact same constellation on the sky can return. Always there is something new. This fact is very important for any horoscope to take into account.

It is spoken about ‚the seven planets‘, as it is spoken about ‚the seven days of the week‘ (or of creation). But still: this ‚Seven-ness‘, be it that ‚of days of the week‘ (or of creation), or be it that ‚of the planets‘, is only a part of a greater ’10-ness‘: just as there are the 8th, 9th and 10th day of SALVATION, too, after the seven of creation, there also are an 8th, 9th and 10th planet beside the 7 visible ones. So the ‚Seven‘ generally only represents the ‚visible‘ part of a greater wholeness. This is also illustrated in the Sephiroth spoken about in the third part of this introduction, where it was said that the 7 Sephiroth actually are only the seven lower ones, while 3 upper Sephiroth are ‚before (visible) creation‘ already.

The 7 is to be experienced as ‚the way‘, whereon the 8, 9 and 10 are not yet visible.

At this point we should look at another distinctive aspect of the Hebrew approach to Astrology in general, which illustrates its opposition to the ‚Babylonian‘ or any other ‚worldly‘ approach. It

140

concerns the actual ‚dating' of the (lunar) months, which are ruled by the respective zodiacal signs. These lunar months in the Hebrew approach are only counted from the day on, when at least ‚two witnesses' proclaim to have sighted the crescent of the New Moon. And these two witnesses have to be independent from each other. By this method it is made sure that ‚the human factor' is integrated into the calculation and that this human factor is established even as having a certain 'superiority over time' in this world; ‚Mankind decides, what is counted to have happened in this world' – from a one-sided rational point of view this may sound strange, even crazy … but it is the case nevertheless for human reality. And the fact that it shall be ‚two witnesses, independent from each other', who have to testify for the new moon sighting, bears the deeper meaning that this method of judging represents the insight that the two sides of reality (the appearing and the hidden) are independent from each other and only can be (and have to be) brought together by Mankind.

This 'not taking into account' of the human factor, that humanity indeed is a decisive factor in the ongoing of this whole creation, is the main reason, why all the ‚babylonian' approaches to Astrology mostly fail actually at some point. They are only calculating with ‚the steady', with the perfectly calculateable. But that is, like ‚looking at the light of the Moon as identical with the light of the Sun, and at the light of the Sun as identical with the eternal Light of Creation …'

The order of the days of the week with their

141

planetary correspondences is nothing which could be explained astronomically, by 'natural science', because there is no such order of the planets like in the week's days. But in the mythical realm there indeed is such an order: we know it as the ‚7 days of creation' (Sun, Moon, Mars, Mercury, Jupiter, Venus and Saturn).

In the english language the planet's ‚popular' names (which are – except for Sun and Moon – the Roman/Latin versions of these names) are not so visible anymore in the naming of the week's days (accept for Sun, Moon and Saturn: Sunday, Monday, Saturday), because the germanic languages use names of certain ‚gods' of the germanic/nordic pantheon instead, which were perceived as corresponding to the Roman names of the planets (which were seen as ‚gods', too, by the ancient Germanians as well as by the Romans). But in the french or italian language for example the planets from ‚tuesday' until ‚friday' are still better traceable as stemming from the original Roman pantheon: Mardi/Martedi, Mercredi/Mercoledi, Jeudi/Giovedi, Vendredi/Venerdi (= Mars-day, Mercury-day, Jupiter-day and Venus-day).

Now, when we begin describing the planets one after another, it should always be considered that the visible lights on the sky do not represent firstly ‚themselves' in the perspective of the Hebrew Astrology, but they represent certain aspects of reality. The Sun on our sky for example does not represent solely this one lightest light on the sky which is bringing the brightness of the day on Earth, but this visible Sun represents ‚light' itself, the ‚true

Sun', so to speak, the original, primordial light created on the first day of creation week (which would be the ‚cosmic Sunday'). This ‚true Sun' of the first day is not yet the visible Sun on the sky; the ladder is only created on the 4th day of creation, when the ‚female', the concrete side of it appears.

We will now go through the seven visible planets for a first time, with the ambition to ‚paint a picture' of their respective characteristics, often by means of telling a biblical story dealing with the major topic of this respective ‚level of existence'. And this ‚painting a picture' will be the main section of this fifth part. After that we will try to find some deeper 'systematic' in the character of the single planets, as well as in their specific order from Sun till Saturn and their inter-connectedness.

As already mentioned in the description of the zodiacal sign of Leo, the Hebrew word for 'sun' means 'servant', too. Here we get another layer of this meaning: the Sun 'serves' to show certain things, serves to 'signify' (as the prototype of ALL the planets and stars actually, since they all serve to signify something, being 'signs', like stated on the fourth day of creation in the Bible, see Genesis 1,14).

The mythical Sun, for which the visible one is a symbol in the Hebrew Astrology, is the ‚breakthrough out of chaos', the birth out of the ‚toho wa bohu' of the beginning (a wording in the biblical language of creation week, see Genesis 1,2; meaning something like ‚empty and void', but also translateable as ‚marveling and wondering'!). Thus the Sun is very important for every horoscope. In the horoscope it is the signifier for the basic question, in which sign(s)

143

something fundamentally expresses itself, where it firstly ‚enters reality, existence'. In any beginning of an entity inside this creation of our world, a certain ‚crisis', an individual desperation is present, from that the light and order of this mythical Sun then can come out of, from which it can ‚resurrect' out of. So the Sun stands for ‚Resurrection out of Death', too, as a spontaneous restoration of ‚order out of chaos'.

It is only ‚light' that shows borders, contours, outlines of objects; by this, the light shows ‚order' in creation. That means: even IF there is order already in the dark, it is not seen and thus not perceived as such, we still would stumble over the ‚orderly present things', as long as we do not see them before our feet. Only the light brings the actual experience of order. In this sense the Sun, or rather the light it represents, stands on the beginning of what we call ‚reason', ‚rationality'.

In the horoscope the ‚Sun-sign' is describing the point, where the individual comes into existence out of a pressuring manifoldness of this world, which would be crushing, if it was not brought to a birth finally at this point; it is like the coming together of sperm and ovum in an atmosphere of chaos (in the ‚matrix', the uterus; also compare this correspondence to what was already said about the 9th day and the ‚underworld' being a ‚womb'), when suddenly from then on the inseminated egg begins to orderly develop inside the womb towards unique individual life.

Here we touch an interesting point for a horoscope in the Hebrew tradition. There are actually TWO points of interest, of which the star constellations are looked at: the date of the actual birth AND the date of the conception, too (which is calculated as exactly 271 days backwards from birth, because this is what the numeric value of the word ‚pregnancy' is in Hebrew (‚hareyon': 5-200-10-6-50).

This double perspective on the genesis of an individual (especially concerning the standing of the Sun) is explained with the following: at conception as well as at birth you get ‚redeemed from darkness to light'. And indeed: creation itself IS a redemption; a redemption out of chaos, out of the ‚tohu wa bohu' of the primal state of the world.

In the words of the fourth creation day in the biblical account, the ‚planets' (and the zodiacal signs, too; all the 'stars') are also described as 'signs'. And the letters of a language, especially of the Hebrew, are called 'signs', too (the Hebrew word for the 'signs' in the sense of stars is ‚othoth' and for the signs in the sense of the letters is ‚othioth'). So the stars as well as the letters of a language are signifying something that comes to visibility, which is 'not from here' actually, which is brought into this reality of our world by means of these 'signs'.

The horoscope shows a causality in the seemingly ‚mere coincidence' of your birth at a specific point in time, and of the whole situation you are born into: whether you are born as a Chinese or as a Swiss, as an Azerbaijanian or as a German, is NOT a coincidence at all, but it expresses something out of the harmonic wholeness of creation, which we human beings cannot comprehend in its totality, but which nevertheless is heavily important even unitl down into its assumedly ‚lowest' details.

145

Summarizing it: the Sun is the ‚planet of breakthrough'; in the sign of the Sun there is a breaking through out of chaos, out of death and a bringing to resurrection; it is life born (again) out of corruption. After this initial breakthrough the second, third, fourth stage, and so on, ‚consequently', almost ‚easily' follow after; after the breakthrough out of nothing there begins ‚continuity'. But the breakthrough itself is out of a sudden, compareable to nothing.

The planet Moon represents the happenings on the second day of creation week: the 'separation of the waters above and the waters below'. And here we remember: ‚water' mythically always means ‚time', too. So: from here on there exist two ‚kinds of time', one ‚male time' above, and one ‚female time' below. That is: ‚time' is 'not definite', it is ambiguous; the ‚male time above' is not measurable for us: the '40 years in the wilderness' of the Israelites after the Exodus out of Egypt, or the ‚400 years of slavery in Egypt' are not to be found on our 'normal' calendars or historical timelines. Such a try would be like ‚dressing up a woman as a man, putting onto her the garments of a man' (see the biblical ‚prohibition' of such practices, as well as the other way around, men dressing up as women: Deuteronomy 22,5). Doing such would mean: the woman would not be recognized as being female anymore, possibly leading people astray by this!

What is the most primitive purpose of ‚Woman and Man' in nature? The man shall impregnate the woman – so the ‚male time' spoken of in the stories of the Bible shall impregnate the ‚female time' of our

146

own lives down here. Again we can refer to the New Testament, to the birth of Jesus, to that famous ‚virgin birth‘, to exemplify this principle of the ‚female‘ down here being impregnated by the ‚male‘ from above: Only by the impregnation of the ‚female time of our lives down here‘ by the ‚biblically told male time and the happenings in it‘ we can ‚give birth to the Messiah‘ in ourselves, we can experience salvation in our lives.

In the sign of the Sun, the ‚waters above and below‘ are still together; in the sign of the Moon they are separated. The Moon represents the female principle and is traditionally placed ‚in the left column‘, while the Sun as the male principle is placed ‚in the right column‘. And again concerning this split in ‚male and female‘ in a more principle dimension: in every human being there is equally present BOTH; only the appearence of each individual down here on Earth has a slight tendency to one or another, to male or to female; but spiritually (and that means: ‚actually‘) every human being is clearly ‚male AND female‘, as stated in creation-story in Genesis 1,27: ‚zakhar uneqabah‘ (by the way, a term having the exact same numeric value as the word ’shamayim‘, ‚heavens‘ = 390).

During the last parts of this introduction we already touched on the fact that the Moon is, contrary to the Sun, a symbol of development, of movement, change. The light of the Moon is not the ‚full‘ light of the Sun, like it is only ‚a reflection‘, an indirect kind of light. The same is the case for the ‚left side of the world‘, our world down here, compared to the ‚right side‘, the male aspect of our world, ‚the heavens‘:

147

our light, our understanding down here is always only ‚Moon light‘, indirect. The Sun is active, too. But only from the background, we can perceive it not yet in totality; this will only be the case, as soon as we reach the ‚day half‘ of our day. Now we are still in the ’night half‘.

In a horoscope, the Moon is understood as especially representing the bodily side of existence. The body has its ‚phases‘ like the moon has, the waves of changing moods and feelings. And in the female body this is especially visible: at some times ‚the fruit is likely‘, fertility is high, at some times it is even almost sure; but at other times it is impossible for the body to conceive, then it is ‚renewing itself‘ for a new, fresh cycle. Such is it in any other bodily regard, too, for females as well as for males (only for other bodily functions not as obvious as in the specific female ovulation cycle).

In times of a decreasing Moon our body is weakened, at Full Moon on the other hand it is especially strenghtened. Full Moon even tends to make people kind of ‚over-ambitious‘, carefree; a Full Moon can be perceived as a call to be ‚audacious‘, boldfaced, impertinent even.

But when looking at the Moon and its effect on the human body it must be always remembered: the Moon is NOT the Sun, the Moon ‚always changes‘. So even the root-horoscope may show a certain Moon-state, signifying for example a general bodily weakness – then this is to be understood ONLY as a beginning, it WILL certainly change during the course of life in this world, it will move in waves up and down, to and fro during life, like the Moon itself

148

does in its monthly change of shape and lightness. Beside this, the shape of the Moon at the time of conception of an individual is equally to be drawn into consideration while looking at his/her root-horoscope (due to the symbolic 271 days from conception until birth, this conception-Moon in the monthly lunar cycle is always exactly ‚5 days earlier‘ in its shape than the Moon shape at the day of birth).

There is (or at least used to be) a certain practice in Judaism, but in other ancient cultures, too: no name is given to an illness of the body, to a disease somebody is suffering of. Because the naming of it would ‚fixate‘ it. It is okay to state that the respective man or woman is ’not doing so well right now‘ in his/her bodily condition, and of course it can be talked about the symptoms and searched for reasons and possible healing methods – but no definite name is given to the state of the ill person. In contrary: rather it is given a new name to the ill person him- or herself, with an explanation like: Under your old name, yes, you ARE really in a bad condition. But now you get a new name, a ’new essence‘, and a new beginning this shall be for you! ... and by this practice the illness indeed (sometimes) can be coped with in surprisingly effective new ways.

In the Hebrew Astrology that specific point in the lunar cycle, when the Moon completely disappears into the darkness for one to two nights, the so-called ‚New Moon‘, is understood as a symbol of the moment of dying. And by this, it shows that ‚dying‘ is actually a renewing!

Not a surprise: biblically New Moon is recommended to be celebrated as a feast day; it is called ‚rosh

149

chodesh' in Hebrew, literally ‚head of the month, head of the moon', and ‚moon' would be even more literally translated as ‚the (re-)new(ing one)'. And the word for ‚head' (‚rosh') is the same as the word ‚principle'; so the whole name of the feast of New Moon can be translated more abstractly as the ‚principle of renewing'. And this ‚principle of renewing', which is celebrated in the feast, expresses itself in this world of the seventh day as what we perceive as ‚Death'.

This symbolic ‚moment of dying' is not meant to be ONLY speaking of the actual ‚bodily' death. Especially it refers also to any great ‚revolution' in your life's circumstances, essential changes in your perspectives on life. And every moment in life is a little bit of ‚dying' anyway …

In this world of ours, in physical nature around us, all 'seed' is always ‚a wasting of potential'. Because the very most of the 'seeds' (the seeds of plants, as well as the semen of animals and sperm of human beings) will ‚die' without ever bringing fruit, just corrupting in infertile grounds. But in the Ancient Wisdom this fact of nature is commented: Well, yes – but in other levels of reality, all these ‚lost' seeds DO bring fruit; this world here is NOT only meant for itself, but it has an effect on uncountable other realities, too! So nothing is ‚wasted' here, even if it may seem like that sometimes (or even very often …). What corrupts and gets lost HERE, will live nonetheless on another level of existence. We may be remembered of the symbol of a burning down candle here, which we mentioned in the third part dealing with the male signs, when the sign of Virgo was introduced.

150

The beginning of a biblical ‚day‘ is always in the night half of that day (see Genesis 1). We now still are living in the bodily realm, where ‚the moon is ruling and reigning‘: we only see ‚indirectly‘, the light of the mythical Moon is our only enlightening lamp in this world. The mythical Sun IS having its effect in all of it – but solely from the background for now. The light of the Moon only enlightens to a certain degree; when the actual ‚day‘ with the Sun will break through, then we will finally see reality in all clarity.

Mars is the third of the seven planets, so the corresponding day of creation week is the third day. By now it should be exhaustingly established that the ‚third in a row‘ always is of a ‚twin character‘. In the case of creation week this means: on the third day (as well as later also on the 'second third‘, the sixth day) we have two creation-deeds, two words of God beginning with ‚it shall be …‘. On the ‚day of Mars‘ the dry land is becoming visible after the waters assemble to ‚one spot‘; and plant life emerges, that is: ‚growth‘, a first form of ‚life‘ begins on the dry land.

Iron, the typical metal of swords and weapons, is traditionally perceived as the ‚Mars-metal‘; and Mars has indeed to do with ‚war‘, with battle and with fight. But it would be far too simplified to see in Mars only a ‚god of war‘, especially when we understand the word ‚war‘ only in the very material, worldly sense.

A very important aspect of the stage of ‚Mars‘ is: it is the ‚day of the child‘: the ‚father‘ is the first day, the ‚mother‘ is the second day, and then the child appears in the middle of them both (see again the ‚Sephiroth‘-

151

scheme in the third part of this introduction, where the third Sephirah also appears under the first two in a centric position). The ‚child' thereby is having something of both parents integrated inside itself. So is the character of ‚planet Mars', too: it integrates the ‚male', eternal, steady character of the first day (the ‚dry land'), as well as the ‚female', timely, changing character of the second day (the ‚ocean') to something new (the actual ‚earthly landscape', as we know it, with both: dry lands AND waters).

Namely ‚the two trees' appear on this third day. The ‚tree' is in the mythical world always to be grasped as a symbol for growth, for development, for the experience that ‚from the other side something is growing into appearance here'.

The ‚Tree of Knowledge (of Good and Evil)' means: something is challenging Mankind to form an opinion on the things which are visible, touchable, senseable; but while doing so, still not necessarily to JUDGE (only) after those factors! We should be seeing the crucial side of the things nevertheless in the other half of reality, in the ‚qualitative', instead of the ‚quantitative'.

But well, as we know from the further happenings of the story … Mankind choses the ‚Moon World', the world of quantity, of change and development, of causal chains – and by this, the ‚long path' (remember the sign of Libra …) begins for us.

There are especially two basic types of people in the sign of Mars: the extrovert and the introvert. The former is directly fascinated by the appearing things, he is feeling good in this ‚world to touch'. The ladder

152

on the other side is feeling always a little bit ‚wrong here‘ in this world, he is never arriving completely in this world, prefers 'staying a guest‘ here.

But BOTH parts of character should be experienced in oneself, both should learn to know each other, become a unity inside the human being! That is the actual ‚war‘ in Mars: introvert versus extrovert. This battle could be a respective longing for the other side of character (like a desire to ‚capture‘ that other side for oneself), or it could be a feeling of being irritated by the mere possibility of coming in contact with the other side (and thus the wish to ultimately get rid of ‚the enemy‘); then there of course will be an inner (and sometimes even an outer) conflict, aiming to destroy the respective other side. It is not so much the question here, WHICH of the two sides of character is the stronger present inside you. The crucial factor is the way how the two sides in yourself are able to connect to each other.

The ‚third day‘ is characterized as the point, where ‚the two first days‘ come to confrontation: as the ‚hidden‘ (spiritual) beginning of creation (of ‚the world‘, as well as of ‚yourself‘) being confronted with the ‚appearing‘ (physical) beginning of it (a conflict represented in Jacob and Esau, as already discussed in the sign of Gemini). But there is no decision yet, in this world (also like in the life-long confrontation of Jacob and Esau, where the decision happens only in another realm, ‚in the Angel-fight at the Jabbok-river‘, and only is expressed in certain happenings ‚on the ground‘ afterwards, as ‚Esau not being able to actually fight Jacob, making peace with him – but still not beginning to live together with him

153

in one land').

And one fact should be stressed: This confrontation in the sign of Mars is nothing bad. In Judaism there is even a tradition to celebrate a wedding specifically on this third day of the week (that is: on ‚Tuesday'). It is explained: when the opposition is at its strongest, the coming together of an opposite should be celebrated! Then ‚the two trees' are connected again, and the connection becomes ‚the path' on which we achieve to experience indeed ‚the hidden integrated into the appearing'!

We shall long and desire for this uniting of the opposites in any regard, when we are under the challenging influence of an inner conflict in this sign of the planet Mars.

Mercury, as the 4th planet, is in tight connection with the first one, with the Sun. The ancient and medieval ‚alchemists' are said to have desired to ‚make gold' with Mercury's help; in this we can see that there indeed WAS some kind of understanding of the connection between the fourth and the first, between Mercury and the Sun (because the specific metal corresponding to the Sun is ‚gold', like iron corresponds to Mars and silver corresponds to Moon). Only these medieval alchemists (or at least many of them) may have been a little bit too fixated solely on the material expression of spiritual truth, searching more for benefit inside this world than for their connection back to the Source of all Being … But let us not forget: Our modern scientific discipline of ‚chemistry' has its historical origins in exactly this ‚alchemy' of the medieval era (bringing us inventions like ‚porcelain/chinaware' and ‚black powder').

154

In Hebrew the name of the fourth planet is ‚kokhav‘, basically meaning just 'star‘ in the broadest sense; and on the 4th day indeed all the (‚physically visible‘) stars are made, according to the biblical account of creation week (see Genesis 1,14-18).

So on ‚Mercury's day‘ the ‚original light‘ of the first day gets into appearance in the physical realm; we could say: there is a ‚concretisation‘ on this fourth day (remember: the 4 is perceived as the number of the ‚female‘, of the ‚concrete‘).

With Mercury ‚a new message‘ comes into the world: the message expressed in the 'signs‘ of the sky, the ‚message of the stars‘, as it is written: ‚the heavens are proclaiming the glory of God‘ (Psalm 19,1). That is why biblically it is Moses, who is associated with this planet: Moses, the bringer of the message of redemption out of Egypt's enslavement, and of the message of ‚God's will‘, given to His people at Mount Sinai, beginning with the so-called '10 Commandments‘ (Exodus 20,1ff). We can say that with the mythical ‚Moses‘ in this world the ‚public‘ knowledge of ‚the Word (of God)‘ begins. Equally, the planet Mercury in a horoscope can signify the ‚direction‘ (= the zodiacal sign in which it stands), from where this 'new message‘ is (primarily) reaching the individual human being under this constellation as a 'second breakthrough‘ in life.

In ancient mythology Mercury or ‚Hermes‘ is primarily just ‚the messenger‘ (of ‚the gods‘) – Moses is more than only a messenger, he is himself the leader out of captivity, too, bringing the children of Israel until the border of the ‚Promised Land‘. INTO this Promised Land it will be only ‚Joshua‘

(same Hebrew name in the original language as ‚Jesus') who leads them.

There is a strong connection between Moses and the famous prophet Elijah (for Elijah's story, see 1 Kings 17,1 – 2 Kings 2,18): both are messengers of ‚good news'. Beside this, Elijah is said to 'never have died' (but to ‚have been taken away alive' from this Earth by God); so, it is explained, the messenger of Good News ‚does not know death', has 'never tasted the grave' – he lives eternally.

On the 4th day, like on the 1st, happens a breakthrough, too. The second 3 days are a repetition of the first three on a higher level. On the end of the 3rd day there is established the opposition of ‚the two trees'; and we know: Mankind is going to be taking of the ‚wrong tree', thus being in danger to ‚get lost for ever', perishing in the manifoldness of creation. But with the 4th day now there begins the impact of the ‚direction back' being shown. And connected with this 4th day is 'netzach', the name of the fourth of the 7 Sephiroth, meaning ‚victory' (see part 3). On the fourth day it is not a breakthrough out of nothing, out of chaos (like in the beginning on the first day), but it still is a breakthrough: one out of the feeling of being lost, a sudden liberation out of captivity.

Mercury brings the good news, it is the 'star' which is showing, ‚how far we are', where we stand (and what has to come now, to not get lost). We can compare this to a certain passage in the New Testament: a 'star' is leading the ‚wise men', the ‚magicians', to the new born Jesus (see Matthew 2,2+9ff).

156

The Hebrew word ‚kokhab' has a numeric value of 42 (20+20+2); and there are exactly 42 generations listed in the beginning of the gospel of Matthew, thereby describing ‚the physical development' from Abraham until Jesus (see Matthew 1,1-17). So Jesus ‚fulfills' this '42'. And the 'star', which the magicians observe, finally stands still over the location where Jesus is born.

And it is also exactly 42 stations on the wandering of the children of Israel through the wilderness after their exodus out of Egypt under the leadership of Moses (see Deuteronomy 33,3-49).

‚Hermes', the greek version of Mercury, is said to be the ‚hurrying messenger' with ‚wings on his shoes and his helmet'; and the metal associated with this fourth of the planets is ‚quicksilver' (indeed traditionally called by the name ‚mercury'/'mercurius', too): a metal, so fluid and thus ‚quick', we cannot really grasp it as a metal …

The planet Jupiter, representing the fifth day of creation week, is called ‚tzedeq' in the Hebrew tradition, which means ‚justice; just, righteous'. We already thoroughly looked at this concept of the ‚Tzaddiq', the ‚Proven One' or ‚Wise One', which actually is associated with the ‚tzade', the ‚fishhook' as the tool to ‚fish out the fish out of the water-world up to the dry land', symbolically referring for the ability of the ‚Proven One' to bring someone to an experience of Eternity (see again the paragraph about Pisces in the second part of this introduction).

And on the fifth day animal life appears: birds flying up to the firmament, fish swimming down in the

157

waters of the earth. So finally life is created as something moving freely in space, not ‚only‘ the steady plant life (like it is present since day 3), but now the warm and cold blood of birds and fish is bringing this movement towards both vertical directions, up and down.

‚Blood is a very special juice‘, how the famous german poet Goethe once wrote … Blood is connecting the organs of a living body to a unity of the whole organism. And in the Hebrew language the word for ‚blood‘ is ‚dam‘, which is derived from the verb ‚domeh‘, meaning ‚to be similar, resemble‘; thus it is especially the blood, which is making the ‚resemblance of God‘ in any form of life – but especially later in human life. Like God's presence in His creation is connecting every single part of this manifold world of nature to one united wholeness, it is the blood in a body that is connecting the organs, all the single cells to one united organism.

The so-called ‚Lord's Supper‘ of the New Testament (see for example Matthew 26,17ff; 1 Corinthians 11,23ff) is to be understood from this point of view, too: the wine as the blood, connecting all the servants of the living God, the disciples of Jesus, with each other, like they are organs of one whole great organism, the ‚Body of Christ‘ (see for example 1 Corinthians 12,12ff).

And to stay in this picture: What has NO connection to the wholeness of the body through a healthy flowing of blood, will die, it corrupts and becomes even a danger for the rest of the body, so that it must be amputated to save the healthy rest of the body (see John 15,1ff).

158

So in this fifth planet and its corresponding day of creation week, ,the blood appears', and ,connects', brings new (forms of) life. In a similar way, on this 5th place of the Sephiroth-scheme, Aaron appears, to ,give Moses an appearance': Aaron is used ,as Moses' mouth' (because Moses himself is 'not a good speaker', as he says of himself; see Exodus 4,10-16), Aaron is the ,left side' pronouncing, what on the ,right side' is implemented; so again we have this harmonic complementarity of male and female principle, of right and left column. When the Bible states ,Moses speaks', it means actually: Aaron speaks FOR Moses; although it still IS Moses who essentially speaks, only now the appearance of Aaron is expressing it for us ,down here', in this world of form and matter.

This is a fundamental principle to be understood: life on this ,left side', in this ,Moon World', can only express what is there already on the ,right side', in the ,eternal blueprint' of time and space reality. So the ,life of the blood, of the physical body' on the 5th day is seen as the corresponding ,left side' of the 'stars, sun and moon' on the 4th day, being the ,right side'; and THAT is exactly, why ,Astrology' has its right to exist – because moving life on the physical Earth is indeed the expression of the movements of the stars in the sky.

Like the 1st and the 4th day (and planet), also the 2nd and the 5th day (and planet) have a strong connection: Jupiter can be seen as a repetition of the Moon on another level. The Moon (its shape during the lunar cycle and its place in the zodiacal signs) builds the foundation of the appearance of your body; then

159

Jupiter determines the actual life of that body, the movement of the body through the surrounding world, its connectedness to the cycles and circumstances of nature around you.

In every human being both is present: the movement of the birds, and the movement of the fish; like the both ‚waters‘, both kinds of time, the ‚lower‘ AND the ‚upper‘ time, are present in the life of all of us. And the connection of both sides is being mediated by the stars. Here we should remember what has been said about the ‚two souls‘ of Mankind (see the first part of this introduction), of the ‚divine soul‘ and the ‚animal(istic) soul‘: between both souls there are the zodiacal signs with the planets as ‚the spirit‘, ‚ruach‘, that mediates, and brings the messages from the ‚divine‘ root of our being down to the ‚animalistic, earthly‘ existence of our body.

Important questions for a horoscope concerning this fifth planet are: Which side, the ‚bird‘ or the ‚fish‘, is stronger inside you? Or is there already the perfect equilibrium?

How is Mercury coming into play, as the right side, the heavenly source of the bodily processes? What about the Moon, as the foundation of your bodily appearance? Such questions help finding out strenghts and weaknesses of the human being under the influence of a certain constellation.

The biblical ’sacrificial system‘ is to be grasped from this astrological point of view as a detailed description of the Jupiter-aspects of human life; ‚animals‘ to be ’sacrificed‘ are thus representing certain bodily functions and body parts to be applied as ‚qurban', for specific ‚approaches' to the Eternal. The biblical book of Leviticus is from this perspective indeed a ‚book of human anatomy' – only not described it from the physical side, from the side of ‚Becoming', but from the point of view of the ‚Being', describing the conditions of human bodily life ‚from the other side'.

Venus, the planet of the sixth day, is called 'nogah' in the Hebrew tradition, a word meaning something like 'shining; appearing one'. And as we know, Mankind is created on this sixth day; Mankind is thus practically ‚appearing' through the influence of this sixth planet – just as Mankind's more abstract ‚possibility' in general, ‚in principle', Mankind's theoretical potential, is rooted (as something 'steady') in the zodiacal sign of Virgo (see part three again for the details). Under the influence of Venus now the individual human being actually appears, is ‚born into the world' as one unique single entity (and thus is not so 'steady' anymore, as abstract humanity is ‚in principle', but now being rather ‚fluctuant' in his/her concrete state of being).

By means of Venus the individual human being can express itself well in this world of the appearing, and it can easily be known by the surrounding world. This brings forth certain negative consequences, too …

As we know well, ‚the snake' does appear on this 6th day, beginning to speak to the human, and to be more precise: to its ‚female', to its ‚appearing side' – and by this, the LONG path begins. This long path, which on the first glance is looking like it will end in a total perishing of the individual through ‚death'. But still:

161

in the very end there WILL be the ‚return home'
nevertheless. And then even with the priceless
additional joy of having regained something already
thought to be lost for ever!

But we cannot deny: ‚Where the snake speaks to
Mankind, the long, rough journey begins' …

In the sign of Venus a human being CAN find some
sympathy of the surrounding world, but almost even
more likely it will be, that the individual inflicts upon
him- or herself the antipathy of the ‚adversary side':
in the sign of Venus every doing of good, every
unselfish GIVING, is NOT being appreciated by the
world, the world paradoxically even ‚gets angry' for
being granted such an unselfish gift.

So on the one side, in the sign of Venus the
possibility is experienced, that ‚giving yourself away
completely' is indeed possible – but also on the other
side it is experienced, that this ‚giving yourself away'
can trigger the horrific anger of the one receiving this
gift. It is like God giving Himself away totally for the
purpose of original creation (‚out of nothing'): the
world just cannot appreciate this ineffable gift, even
hates God for it unconsciously.

A bad positioning of Venus thus can bring aggression
and anger against a being under this constellation;
but explicitly NOT as a consequence of ‚bad deeds'
commited by that being, but exactly as a response to
the GOOD ones. And still: in the end, the long
suffering will lead to the ‚happy ending' of the story,
even making clear, that it HAD to come like this.

The biblical figure of Joseph (who is associated with
this general 'sixth' of the seven, with the 6th planet,

6th day and 6th Sephirah) shows us some aspects of this phenomenon: Both, from his brothers as well as in Egypt, Joseph is attacked because he is doing good, doing the right things, because he is honest.

Let's imagine for a moment what possibly would have happened, if he would have been more 'normal', and would have „just given in' to the wishes of the world around him …

For instance, in the one crucial situation, when the wife of his master Potifar in Egypt tries to seduce him to adultery (Genesis 39,7-20) – what would have been, if Joseph would have done with her, what she desired? From the ongoing of the story as we know it we must say: it was very good, that Joseph stayed honest, that he did not let her seduce him, and that he in consequence got innocently accused for doing it – because exactly by this, Joseph in the end becomes the great interpreter of dreams in prison, and by means of that, since Josephs dream-interpreting art finally becomes known to Pharao, Joseph becomes even the second mightiest man in Egypt after Pharao. But it is of course a looong way until then, with much suffering for Joseph, he is forced to spend many years in captivity, being forgotten in there and as so often: being under-estimated (compare this to what was said about Virgo in the third part, too).

We typically ask here: why HAS to be at first that whole long way with all the suffering? Why can't it be good from the beginning on?

As already seen, here in Venus we have a reflection of the sixth zodiacal sign: here, too, the ‚olive has to be picked first' (= the growth in this world has to

163

have an end), before it gets pressed and can give the oil for the 8th day of anointment of Messiah. This ‚anointing‘ to come IS a sure thing, ‚on the 8th day‘. On the 6th day nevertheless there must be a perishing first.

Now we want to look at another interesting aspect of this ‚6th out of the 7′: the planet Venus is associated with the ‚hind‘, that is the ‚female deer‘; and it is specifically interpreted as ‚the hind on the late night sky‘, the ‚hind of the morning‘ (in Hebrew: ‚ayeleth ha shakhar‘), as what western world would call the ‚morning star‘.

In this sense Venus is an important sign of redemption: the suffering that is being experienced until the end is suddenly understood as evidence of the own devotion!

But this sentence probably has to be explained in some more detail: It is the same principle like that in which the world is created: God gives Himself away for the world totally, He draws Himself back ‚into a nothingness‘, thereby making space for the world to exist; and exactly this drawing back and giving Himself away totally is experienced by the world, which is created through this act of devotion, as a suffering – because it is not known as such, nor acknowledged, nor appreciated.

But let us look a little deeper into this picture of the ‚morning hind‘. The famous Psalm 22 in Hebrew begins with the words: ‚la menetzeach al ayeleth ha shakhar‘, usually translated as ‚to the chief musician, upon the morning hind‘. But ‚la menetzeach‘ stems from the word ’netzach‘, the word for ‚victory‘ in the

164

sense of the fourth Sephirah, thus meaning a ,victory in the breaking through'. So ,la menetzeach al ayeleth ha shakhar' should be translated more appropriately as ,to the winning one on the morning hind'. And then, still in the first verse of that Psalm 22, there follow the famous words ,Eli, Eli lama azabthani?', ,my God, my God, for what purpose have you forsaken me?', which Jesus is told to have cried out hanging on the cross, citing this verse of the Psalms.

Now the symbol of the ,hind', too, should be elaborated on a little bit more: the (male) ,deer', in Hebrew ,tzevi' or ,tz'vi', is typically combined with the name ,David', when this name ,David' is given to jewish children. That is the case, because traditionally King David, as the prototype for the expected redeemer and saviour, is associated with the deer – and that again is, because the deer is associated with great speed, agility. So the name combination ,Dawid Tzvi' actually means: ,Dawid' (= the Beloved One, the Messiah, the Redeemer and Saviour) is so fast, He is already nearer as you think! And especially when applied in this sense to the Messiah as a symbol of (the experience of) Salvation, it is explained: the Messiah, although from the beginning of the world already 'sitting to the right hand of the Father in Heaven', is also already down here with us all the time, and He will be again ,at His Fathers right hand in Heaven' in the end. HE, and with Him, the 'salvation' he represents, is so ,quick' that it happens before we can grasp it; it is in the future, but already here. He ,binds the beginning and the end together', making it one unity, inseparable. This 'speed' of the Messiah, of salvation, is

165

symbolically expressed in the picture of the deer and the hind, because these animals are for the human eye very fast and disappear in a moment, as soon as they realize to be seen by anyone.

The ‚morning star‘ appears, when the night is in her darkest hour. But it is the time when the night is beginning to come to an end, too. Remember the story of Adam and the terror he feels, after he lost the Paradise, when he is experiencing the first night (see again part three of this introduction) … This darkest hour of the night, right before the ‚Hind of the Morning‘ appears out of the blackness of the sky as the relieving sign of a soon ending of this thick darkness – this darkest hour is a tough test for Mankind in many regards, be it in its symbolic associations, be it in the very ‚hard physical‘ facts of life: For statistically it is proven that in the darkest hour of the night the ‚death rate‘ of people significantly increases. Like their heart is feeling at this point of the night: oh, it is sooo dark, if this darkness won’t come to an end right now, I cannot survive this! As a consequence from the Ancient Wisdom it is thus recommended, especially for the practice in hospitals, to have no surgeries in the darkest hour of the night (if possible – emergencies of course excluded from this rule), between around 5 and 6 a.m.

The Hebrew word ’shakhar‘ means ‚early morning‘, as well as it means ‚black‘ – so in the language there is a strong consciousness for the fact that the early morning actually begins exactly at the darkest point of the night.

The ‚ayeleth ha shakhar‘ is an instrument, too,

similar to a harp. And a ‚mizmor‘, a ’song‘ (we are still looking at the very first verse of that 22nd Psalm), is actually derived from ‚zamar‘, meaning ‚grapevine‘ (as already mentioned above, the symbol of wine often refers to ‚blood‘, especially as ‚connecting all the organs of an organism‘, see the paragraph concerning Jupiter; and see the 15th chapter of the biblical Gospel of John, too). So a true ’song‘ in this Hebrew sense of ‚mizmor‘ is connecting us with all that exists, like the wine, and like the blood; and especially it connects ‚the Beloved One (= dawid)‘ with all creation.

The ‚Eli, Eli‘ that follows now is traditionally interpreted as referring to the ‚double nature of an experience of the Eternal‘: two times ‚my God‘ it says, once ‚here in the appearing‘, and once ‚in the hidden side of life‘; and this God in both His possibilities of experiencing Him is experienced in this Psalm as having ‚completely forsaken‘ us … ‚Lamah azabthani?!‘ For what purpose?!

In these words Jesus experiences what seems to be the great ‚miscalculation‘ of the Eternal One: the world does not appreciate the love God is giving her, so that God is being rejected by this world, by His own beloved creation (so the ‚Fallen Ones‘, Azazel and Semchasi, seem to have been indeed ‚right‘ in their assumption concerning the ungratefulness of God's most honoured creation …). But: this experience of being rejected for the love one is willing to give is nothing ‚worthless‘ either. Like God took on Himself this rejection by His most beloved creature, to experience the even greater joy of nevertheless being appreciated in the end after all the rejection – so is Mankind offered the opportunity now to experience this aspect of being made ‚in the resemblance of the Eternal‘, too.

And in the sign of Venus it becomes clear finally: IF a human being experiences THIS, to ’stand at the abyss‘ and to see his/her own desperate lonliness in this regard – and IF he or she can BEAR that feeling … then (and ONLY then) salvation can happen.

Let us not forget that the ’sixth fruit‘ is the olive, which has to be pressed to give her precious oil necessary for the ‚anointment‘ of the ‚Anointed One‘ (= ‚Messiah‘, ‚Christ‘). And by the way: the olive, contrary to the first five fruits, has only ONE core, one seed, not many seeds. There is only this ONE way leading to true salvation, to true ‚fruit‘.

Beautiful and shining is the human being in this sign of his/her (actual) appearing to the surrounding world; like Joseph is described (as the only male figure in the Bible) as ‚handsome in form and handsome in appearance‘ (Genesis 39,6; instead of ‚handsome‘ a more literal translation here would be indeed ‚beautiful‘, meaning originally something like ‚to radiate one’s inner light as a shining splendour into the surrounding world‘). And this is the purpose of the suffering: to still ’shine‘, radiate splendour, while experiencing to be cruelly rejected, by this, becoming a living testimony to the surrounding world for the fact that Mankind indeed IS made in the resemblance of the Eternal, being capable of essentially the same divine grace like He grants it to us.

To come to an end now of the description of this very

important one of the seven planets, we summarize: the sign of Venus WILL bring salvation, but especially by the experience of being rejected and innocently attacked. That is a necessary step when coming closer to the end of the path through this world, following the trail ‚out of it‘, approaching the Source of All, as bringing the own actual physical existence as a ‚qurban‘, while staying amongst the surrounding fellow human beings, who are not understanding this ambition and are not WANTING to get involved – not even by receiving the gift of being loved.

The last of the seven planets, corresponding to the last of the seven days, to the ‚Sabbath‘, is Saturn, or in Hebrew ‚Shabtai‘ (meaning something like ‚ending one; sabbathical‘). In every more worldly, ‚babylonian‘ approach to astronomy, Saturn is typically seen very negative. But in the Hebrew perspective on it this is not necessarily the case. Like always, it depends on whether we look at it ‚holistically‘, from both sides of reality, or only one-sidedly. So any negative look on Saturn and its influence in the horoscope is only half of the truth.

On this seventh day ‚of Saturn‘, in this 'stage' of the world we live in now, while ‚God is resting‘, Mankind COULD experience that the world indeed ‚is very good‘ (as stated by God Himself in Genesis 1,31). But there is a strange ambiguity on this 7th day: it is a resting as a preparation for being saved afterwards, for being redeemed out of this world. But it is very hard to accept this ‚resting‘ to be necessary …

169

The name of the 7th ,fruit of the Promised Land' is the ,date', in Hebrew ,thamar' (we already looked at this fruit, and especially at this Hebrew word for the fruit, in the context of the male sign of Libra in the third part). And ,Thamar' also is the name of a biblical figure (actually not only of one, but let us look at only the first of them for now; see Genesis chapter 38):

This woman with the name of Thamar appears as the wife for Judah's son(s): Firstly she gets married to Judah's firstborn called Er; but he ,was evil in the eyes of the Lord' and dies. So Thamar is given instead to Judah's second oldest son, to Onan; but Onan does not want to give ,his' sons for being raised under the name of his brother Er (because this would have been the case according to the biblical recommendations, when they are reduced to the superficial interpretation of the so-called ,levirate marriage'), so Onan ,is spilling it down to the earth', everytime when he is going to Thamar (that is, he deliberately avoids to impregnate her, engaging in a form of ,contraception'); he only wants ,his seed' to be in THIS world, as an earthly ,gain', bearing ,his name', not as ,heavenly fruit' realized in this world down here as something for the benefit of 'someone else'.

By the way: This whole episode of Onan is not to be understood in the modern ,psychological sense' as condemning ,masturbation' or any form of ,contraception', or more general, as condemning the ,wasting of seed' in any form (we already mentioned the apparent ,wasting' of seed in all living nature, that nevertheless is having its purpose from a spiritual point of view).

The third (and at this point the last one) of Judah's sons, is Shelah. And Judah does not want to give him to Thamar, because Judah is afraid that Shelah may die, too, like his two older brothers (‚because' of Thamar, as Judah may be thinking at this point …).

And what happens next is the crucial point of this biblical story: Thamar hides herself under a veil, sits on the road side and waits for Judah; he comes along, thinks she is a ‚prostitute' (paradoxically literally called a ‚Holy One' on many scriptures of the Bible …) – and goes to her for the promise of ‚one little goat from the flock'; and he is leaving a pawn there (his staff, his ring and his girdle). But when he tries to bring her the promised ‚little goat' afterwards as payment, he cannot find her.

Then some time later, in the household of Judah there is a scandal happening: Thamar, the widow, is pregnant! That cannot be, she must have committed adultery!! So Judah wants to let her burn to death for that 'sin' in his eyes. But she shows him the pawn, the staff, ring and girdle he left her, and says: the owner of these things is the father of my unborn child! And at that point Judah understands and sees, that HE is the unrighteous one in the whole story, because he denied her the right to marry his last living son! So he forgives her, lets her live – but Judah does not marry her himself.

Thamar then gives birth to twins, and the happening of this birth is told us to be a little bit strange (Genesis 38,28f): first there comes the hand of one of them and they bind a red string to his wrist, but then

171

the arm is retreated and the other child comes out first. And they name the one with the red string attached to his wrist ‚Zerach' (which means 'shining red') and the other one ‚Peretz' (which means ‚breakthrough'); and Peretz becomes the ‚chosen one', he is the one through whom the chain of generations goes on from Adam over Abraham and Judah until King David – and from David of course the Messiah Jesus arrives later on. So Peretz is indeed the ‚breakthrough' during the generation of Judah (when due to the deaths of Judah's sons Er and Onan the danger arose for the ‚messianic lineage' to cease), the one who makes sure that Judah's fate will be fulfilled at the appointed time later on (concerning this ‚fate of Judah' see the prophecy of Judah's father Jacob about him in Genesis 49,8-12; to ‚bring forth the Peacemaker at one day out of his descendants').

So: Er dies, Onan dies, Shelah stays alone and thereby childless – and Zerach's lineage, too, perishes later like his older brothers' (at an occasion in Joshua's times, when the last descendant of Zerach is stealing ‚banned booty' from the Israelites' defeated enemies and gets destroyed by God for doing so; see Joshua chapter 7, the story of ‚Achan, Son of Zerach').

That means: only Peretz with his descendants actually survives; and in this we can see the 1-4-principle again: the ‚four' are important, too, because without them being part of the story and by this, establishing certain circumstances, the fifth, the ‚One' coming along with the four, would not even have existed as such.

Let's look slightly deeper into the character of the

172

‚four' and of the ‚One' in this constellation of Thamar and her husbands: ‚Er' means ‚consciousness', ‚Onan' means ‚power, potency', ‚Shelah' means 'security, rest; to be carefree' – but all of this won't be ‚enough', to bring forth fruit with ‚Thamar'. It is only ‚Judah', meaning ‚praise of God', who – without consciously trying to! – impregnates her in the end and by this finally establishing for himself a lasting lineage of descendants!

So ‚consciousness, potency and security' indeed ARE an important condition in the encounter with ‚the bitterness of this world', with ‚Thamar' (= 'she is bitter'; as the name of the ‚7th fruit of the Promised Land' referring to the ‚bitterness of this world of the seventh day'), for the things happening as they happen – but in the end it is only the purposeless ‚praise of God' that brings the ‚breakthrough' for ‚this bitter world'.

From this biblical story of Thamar and the sons of Judah we learn that it is a ‚fear of the fruit', which bears the potential of a negative effect of the ‚Saturn'-layer in the individual's life. And in this insight we finally have the explanation for the babylonian approach to this seventh planet, looking at Saturn only as something ‚bad' or even ‚evil'. From the babylonian, purely worldly point of view the ‚fruit' is only to be expected as something ‚causal' following regularly out of the happenings of this world, as something appearing IN this world and being FROM this world. If the true fruit now rather comes as something ‚acausal' NOT from this world, threatening the ‚regular', accustomed perception of

173

human reality … then indeed this TRUE fruit will let us tremble in fear of it, as something with the potential to crush our 'normal' everyday life with our worldly hopes and expectations for our future down here …

Thamar in this story comes along as a perfect symbol of THIS world: no real husband, the father of her dying husbands is being unfair to her; and she just LONGS for fruit: for a true husband and for getting children from him. But she is only achieving it on a very unexpected way … not by being ,openly honest', but by ,veiling herself', and by being willing to even DIE trying to achieve fruit, on the way of a ,Holy One' looked at as a ,prostitute' by the surrounding world.

Always when the redemption is feared (and be it only unconsciously), ,the children are getting killed' (see for example the happenings around Jesus' and Moses' birth, when King Herodes and Pharao are trying to kill every male child of a certain age to prevent the rise of the predicted redeemer). And be it in our life today ,only' the ,child in ourselves', that we try to kill …

So the best advice in the sign of Saturn is: Veil yourself, as Thamar does, to achieve fruit in this world of the seventh day!! That means: Become a mystery, a secret! And believe: the world already was created perfect, on ,day 6'; now, on day 7, it just has to be WAITED, waited in patience for the 8th day. Where we try to enforce anything, we fail. Where we try to improve anything inside this world, we will only do damage to it. Our duty is ,only' to behave as the perfectly created human being in the resemblance of the Eternal One. With this ambition we already have PLENTY enough to do with ourselves and can leave the world around us to be just as it is.

Now, after having encountered the seven planets in this more 'story-telling' mode of approach, we can try to find out their stricter systematic structure, which already has been laid a foundation for in the third part of this introduction, as the description of the so-called Sephiroth. Now we will repeat some of the then mentioned aspects of the seven in short keywords and combine them with the characteristics of the seven planets and ‚days‘ established in this fifth part. It will be for every one of the 7 in the following order: name of the planet in english; name of the planet in Hebrew; translation of the Hebrew name; correspondence to creation week (and creation deed); name of the corresponding Sephirah; keyword of the corresponding ‚happening‘ in the Ancient tale of ‚My Father bought me a little Lamb‘ (told in part 3); corresponding biblical figure; corresponding fruit of the Promised Land; traditionally associated metal (with Hebrew name for that metal; and literal translation)

1. Sun; Chamah; ‚Hot One‘; first day of creation (light); chesed; ‚the cat‘; Abraham; Wheath; Gold (zahab; ‚devotion‘)

2. Moon; Levanah; ‚White One‘; second day of creation (firmament; separation between waters above and waters below); geburah; ‚the dog‘; Isaac; Barley; Silver (kheseph; ‚longing, desire‘)

3. Mars; Moadim; ‚Forces/Powers‘; third day of creation (waters assemble to show dry land + dry

175

land brings forth plant life); tiphereth; ‚the wooden stick‘; Jacob/Esau; Vineyard/Grape; Iron (barzel; ‚piercing‘)

4. Mercury; Kokhab; ‚Star‘; fourth day of creation (sun, moon and stars); netzach; ‚the fire‘; Moses; Fig; Quicksilver (no direct mentioning of this metal in the Bible)

5. Jupiter; Tzedeq; ‚Just(ice)/Righteous(ness)‘; fifth day of creation (birds and fish; life in sky and life in water); hod; ‚the water‘; Aaron; Pomegranate; Tin (bediyl; ’separate; dividing‘)

6. Venus; Nogah; ‚Shining One/Appearing One‘; sixth day of creation (land animals, cattle + Mankind as male and female); jesod; ‚the ox‘; Joseph/Zaphenath-Paneach; Olive; Copper/Bronze (nechosheth; ’snakeyness, serpentine‘)

7. Saturn; Shabtai; ‚Ending One; Sabbathical‘; seventh day of creation (finishing of all work, blessing this day and resting of God); malkhuth; ‚the man‘; David; Honey/Date; Lead (ophereth; ‚dustiness‘)

Finally, to tie back this great load of information concerning the seven planets to the ambition to apply it onto an actual horoscope, we should search for the specific meaning of each planet for the individual human being under a certain constellation. So that ‚a certain planet in a certain zodiacal sign‘ can be read as ‚a certain level of existence of the individual (= planet) having a specific challenge by destiny (= zodiacal sign).

The ’specific challenges by destiny‘ represented in

the 12 signs have already been put into a scheme in the very beginning of describing them, namely in part two of this introduction, before starting with the female signs (the ,triangle' of human experience of reality).

Now something similar shall be tried with the seven planets, generally as being the seven basic levels of human existence (as described in the shape of the ,7 Sephiroth'), and in their specific constellation in a horoscope as being the fundamental anchors of an individual by which this individual is connected to several particular signs out of the general wholeness of the 12 signs of the Zodiac.

In general it can be stated: the first three planets represent aspects more regarding the individual in itself; and the second three represent aspects especially regarding the individual in its connection to the surrounding world.

While the Sun is determining the sudden breakthrough of the individual from the spiritual realm INTO existence in this world down here, in Mercury this individual down here is called to find his specific way THROUGH existence in this world. While the Moon is representing the basic physical state of the body IN ITSELF, in the corresponding Jupiter the life of this body in its connection TO ALL OF CREATION and to the cycles of nature is being represented. And while in Mars the conflict ,of the two trees' is played out INWARDLY inside the character of the individual, in Venus the determining conflict is MATERIALIZED in a ,re-enactment' of the fate of God at creation, and therewith this conflict is happening very much ,outwardly', between the

177

individual and the surrounding world.

On this background we perceive the Sun as the most important planet for the basic character of the individual under the constellation looked at, representing the primal breakthrough from non-existence into being.

The Moon we identify as the first impact of a bodily existence, as the potential of a certain form and state of being and of physically experiencing oneself.

Mars we recognize as the decisive factor for the crucial inner conflict between the opposing tendencies inside oneself towards either an inwardly or an outwardly orientation.

Mercury again we perceive as a breakthrough, a breakthrough happening INSIDE this world, calling and leading us towards the ‚path of return‘, to a path of consciousness of a life for the Eternal.

Jupiter then we experience as determining the bodily realization of our consciousness in the physical world, structuring our life and its biological processes according to our respective situation.

Venus finally determines the character of the actual appearing of the individual inside this world as ‚a spiritual being manifest in a body‘, being challenged by the surrounding world and respectively challenging that surrounding world.

Ultimately, Saturn is understood as the way of realization of ‚the fruit‘ in this world: the ‚odd way‘ on which the return back to the source will be essentially accomplished – surprisingly AGAINST all ‚regular‘ assumptions.

The 3 plus 2 plus 1 Hidden Planets in your Horoscope

We have to overcome the visible aspect of the ‚heavens determining our destiny‘ now. That means: Let us look at the ‚hidden, invisible planets‘, representing the remaining days ‚expected to come‘, after the 'seven days of creation week‘: the 8th, the 9th and the 10th day.

It has been established by now: The seven days are represented in the seven visible planets as well as in the so-called seven ‚Sephiroth‘ or 'spheres of existence‘. The 8th day is the reconnection of these 7 back to the original unity of Creation and Creature with the Creator. So for the life- and world-perception of the human individual the crucial sequence of ‚days‘ (or 'stages‘ or 'spheres‘) is, as already introduced in the very fist part of this approach to Hebrew Astrology: the transitional area from our seven days to the three days to come, so especially the three-ness of 6th, 7th and 8th day, represented especially in the three ‚male signs‘ of the Zodiac, which are stressed to be a close unity.

The 'six first days‘ in the biblical account of creation in Genesis 1 are ‚beyond‘ (or if you will: ‚before‘) linear time. So it is meaningless to speculate whether it refers to ‚6 actual days‘, ‚6000 years‘ or ‚6 million years‘ or whatever timely durance we could measure with our means of ‚female time‘ (for this expression see again for example the paragraph concerning the planet Moon in the last part or the paragraph concerning the sign of Virgo in the third part).

Equally, the first six Sephiroth (to be precise: the first

179

six of the ‚lower seven Sephiroth‘, which have been already introduced in part three) are not to be understood as ‚temporally parallel‘ levels of existence, which would thus ‚go parallel‘ to the seventh Sephirah in which we, as physical human beings, actually live with our material bodies. But the first six Sephiroth are ‚playing into‘ the wholeness of the seven Sephiroth, which in their totality are present in our seventh day, as an influence from another side of reality. And since our (self-)’consciousness‘ is located in the 6th sphere, in the Sephirah called ‚yesod‘, it never really can be grasped as ’something‘ being bound to the linear time, but only if understood as a perspective ‚looking at‘ or ‚experiencing‘ this linear time of the seventh day like ‚from the outside‘ (although of course this consciousness of the sixth day and sphere still IS, as all the Sephiroth are, being contained WITHIN this seventh day, too, but here UNCONSCIOUSLY only).

In this sense we always are ’separated‘ from the world, as we are ’self-conscious beings‘. Only ‚there‘ (or ‚then‘), where we ‚let go‘ of this specific (self-)consciuousness of the sixth Sephiran (and this self-consciousness could easily be associated with the ‚opened eyes‘ after the ‚consumation of the forbidden fruit‘ in the story of ‚the tempting serpent‘ in the ‚Garden of Delight and Pleasure‘, Genesis 3,4-7), when we rather not ‚identify‘ with this consciousness, not define ourselves by it, THEN we can actually experience ourselves as being truly ‚a part of the world‘, not at all being (or rather not ‚feeling‘) separated anymore.

So, according to this Ancient language of creation

myth: the human being lives (primarily) in the 6th, 7th and 8th day. Timely existence as ‚a body in this world‘ may be limited to the 7th sphere, where everything concentrates; but his/her consciousness he/she has on the 6th day, and – what for the following elaborations concerning the ‚hidden planets‘ will be of our main interest – his/her longing goes for the 8th day.

Indeed: Every true ‚relation(ship)‘ you have to anyone and anything around you, is a manifestation of such ‚longing‘ towards the 8th, it is a longing for unification, for experiencing the unity of whole creation. On the other hand, every kind of ‚longing‘ or ‚desire‘ in the sense of 'searching for a benefit‘, an ‚aiming only for (‚personal‘) purpose‘, would be what is called ‚fornication‘, an untrue, unhealthy relation(ship), leading astray from the recommended pathway towards the ‚Promised Land‘ of the ‚Eighth Day‘.

Let us look a little bit more deeply into the mythical description of certain happenings of the 'sixth day‘ now; namely into the origin of the manifestation of the ‚two sexes‘ of Mankind, the split into two aspects of existence.

In the biblical story of the making of the Woman out of the original Man(kind) (see Genesis 2,18-25), there is an interesting Hebrew formulation to be found in the original text: God, the Eternal One, is cited as saying, what is usually translated as: ‚It is not good that the man should be alone; I will make him an help meet for him (or sometimes ‚an help like unto him‘)‘. And this ‚help meet for him‘ in a more

181

literal translation would be ‚a help like his (own) counterpart' or more abstract ‚an assistance as (being) his (own) disclosure/revelation'. In Hebrew this wording is ‚ezer ke negdo' and it has the numeric value of exactly 360. In the more mystical traditions this numeric value is understood as a hint to the ‚360 degree' of a whole geometrical circle, therewith referring to the ‚wholeness of the human individual' only to be experienced when you perceive your counterpart as an actual part of yourself.

And the making of the woman, by splitting the ‚androgynous' primordial Man in two halves, only happened after this androgynous Man had proven that he is not ‚getting to know the animals' around him in an intimate sense as parts of himself (the animals, which actually were made for the sole purpose of being the aforementioned ‚help like his counterpart' in the first place, see Genesis 2,19-20). Mankind shall get into a communicating relationship to the surrounding creation, to all life, to get into communication with God Himself on this way. But what happens is only ‚fornication' with the animals, by 'naming' them, that is: ‚giving them a purpose' separated to the wholeness, according to only the apparent aspects of them. That is why God 'splits' Mankind in two.

And in Verse 21 the Hebrew word ‚tzela' actually means 'side' and not ‚rib', as it is usually translated; so it is the whole one SIDE of Mankind, out of which the ‚woman' is made – not just out of one little ‚rib' of the man. And ‚flesh' is put on the place where this half side of his being is taken from Man(kind).

So in the deeper sense of the myth, here we have the

182

description of the genesis of the ‚hidden‘ (‚male‘) and the ‚visible‘ (‚female‘) side of Mankind in general and of every human being in specific. Indeed, the Hebrew words for ‚male and female‘, ‚zakhar u-neqabah‘ (numeric value of 390, just like ‚heavens‘, 'shamayim‘) would be more literally translated as ‚internalization and vault‘ or as ‚(inner) remembrance and (outer) encasement‘.

The existence of a distinction between male and female bodies in the physical appearance from this perspective is ‚only‘ a 'side effect‘, a material expression of the much more basic dualism of male and female PRINCIPLE.

But let us come now to the ‚breaking through to the 8th day‘. How will it happen in your own everyday life? What is a necessary virtue to display on the path towards it?

We already looked at the topic of a ‚going for the lost sheep‘ in the context of the sign of Gemini in the fourth part. It is the story of ‚the good shepherd‘, in this case represented in Mose coincidentally finding the ‚burning bush‘, when on the search for that little lost sheep.

But for your own life it means: YOU are the shepherd; so what is ‚the flock of your sheep‘? Answer: Your whole life it is, and every little part of it, every ‚little sheep‘ of this ‚flock of yours‘, is important. And as the ‚good shepherd‘ you will always go rescue even the one little lost one gone astray, to let nothing be lost for ever on purpose, not even the seemingly ‚less important‘, or 'not worthy‘. And by THAT you will find that ‚burning bush‘ by

183

coincidence someday, where you will meet God, the Eternal One ‚inside this world of the manifold'.

Or to remember the other picture for this trait of character we already mentioned: like Jacob on his way back over the Jabbok river to get the little broken cup, you will have your ‚fight with the Angel of Appearance' – and by this you ‚get blessed', gain your place to be, as ‚the hidden side of yourself', in this world of the appearing things, too.

Actually, there are not only three ‚hidden planets' beside the 7 visible, but there are six hidden planets, making 13 planets in Total, as many as there are zodiacal signs, when counting the ‚hidden thirteenth', too (we mentioned this 13th in the context of the male sign of Scorpio). The six additional planets can be put into an order of 3+2+1: three, making 10 ‚days' out of the 7 visible ‚days' of our material creation; then two more, ‚New Sun and New Moon' of the New Heavens and New Earth of the world in the coming world of the '10th day'; and finally the One never fully graspable ‚thirteenth', the incalculateable rest, so to speak.

One explanation for the fact that there are said to be 12/13 planets in total is: Because ‚the moving' (= those aspects of creation which are dynamic) adapts itself to the 'steady' (= the more static aspects of creation), there must be indeed 12/13 planets in total, like there are 12/13 signs of the Zodiac as the steady background structure for the moving planets.

This is furtherly underlined with a reference to the famous dream of Joseph (Genesis 37,9), where he dreams of ‚Sun, Moon and eleven stars' bowing

184

down before him, and he himself is perceived as the 12th star. And since his name ‚Joseph', in Hebrew ‚yossef', literally means ‚there be another one!', in total there are ‚expected to be' 13 stars, with the 13th 'not realized yet'.

In fact there is seen a correlation between the order of the 12 sons of Jacob/Israel and the order of the 12 zodiacal signs, both counted in the row of their respective ‚appearing'; so it goes: Reuben as Aries, Simeon as Taurus, Levi as Gemini, Judah as Cancer, Dan as Leo, Naphthali as Virgo, Gad as Libra, Asher as Scorpio, Issakhar as Sagittarius, Sebulon as Capricorn, Joseph as Aquarius and Benjamin as Pisces.

The shortest possible explanation of the essence of the 8th, 9th, 10th, 11th and 12th planets would be: 'name, wishes, knowledge, occupation, mission'. But this should be clarified in much more detail during the following paragraphs, by approaching this vital topic in a slow and careful manner. The eighth day of the week in our timely world is, as well as the 13th Planet in the horoscope, representing Eternity, as only shining into this world of time and space, but never really being here completely. Therefore the description of these concepts, too, is only possible in a way of symbolic, mythical language, as ‚painting a picture with words'. One of these pictures already introduced during the last parts is that of the 'seven fruits (of the Promised Land)'. We should now deepen that concept a little bit.

After the seven fruits of Deuteronomy 8,8 (Wheath, Barley, Grape, Fig, Pomegranate, Olive and Date),

185

there is also an ‚eighth' of the fruits of the promised land: the Almond, or Nut.

By the way: The reason, why tradition has added this eighth fruit to the seven biblically mentioned lies in the fact that there is one certain day in Judaism, when the so-called ‚New Year of the Trees' is celebrated, as the symbolic beginning of the annual time of fruits blossoming on trees and other plants in the land. On this feast day the people typically eat the aforementioned seven fruits in one or another form, to praise the abundancy of fruit and food in the nature all around us. And since the almond is the very first tree to blossom in the yearly cycle, its blossoming consequently falls into the time of this ‚New Year of the Trees'. That's why almonds are used to be eaten as well on this feast, and by this they have become an ‚inofficial' eighth fruit in the row, although not explicitly mentioned in the respective biblical scripture. And from the more mystical point of view, this ‚coincidental' addition of an eighth is even very symbolic and expressing a deep truth. But for this deeper sense, the concept of the seven fruits themselves firstly has to be elaborated on, as representing the seven 'spheres of human existence', the ‚Sephiroth'.

The reason, why the specific seven (respectively eight) fruits are seen as representatives not only of the fruits and their trees themselves, but also as symbols for the Sephiroth, as certain levels or spheres of (especially human) existence, is found in one other scripture of the Bible: ‚ki adam etz ha-sadeh' it says in Hebrew; often translated as ‚for the tree of the field is Man(kind)'s life', but literally it

186

just reads ‚because Mankind (or: ‚a single human being‘) is a tree of the field‘ (see Deuteronomy 20,19; the cited words are found in the last part of this verse, as giving the reason why people 'should never cut down any trees with fruits‘, not even as part of a military siege, while engaging in a war against the inhabitants of the land where the trees grow).

We already mentioned the correspondences of the seven fruits with the Sephiroth in the last part, but have not given any detailed reasons for these associations. Without going into all the dephts of it, some of these details shall be named in the following:

Wheat is seen in its property as ‚food for the rich humans‘ or ‚for feast days‘, symbolically it is ‚for the divine soul in us", as being associated with the Sephirah ‚chesed‘, with that inexplicable breakthrough out of the nothing by means of a self-sacrificing love and infinite devotion – the only true nutrition for the divine inside us.

Barley is seen in its characteristic as ‚food for the poor humans‘ or the ‚everyday food‘, and especially as ‚fodder for animals‘; and thus: as ‚the nutrition for the animal soul in us‘, having to deal with the more physical world, the causal chains of the governing law of nature, like represented in the Sephirah ‚geburah‘.

The Grapes of the vineyard are perceived as being defined especially by bringing forth wine as a noble drink, and the wine is seen as ‚bringing joy‘ (see for example Judges 9,13), and by this, the mystical ‚wine‘ is enabling us to develop true excitement, which ‚enleashes our potential‘, bringing our inner traits to the surface in splendor (see the correspondence with the Sephirah ‚tiphereth‘, meaning ‚beauty, splendor‘; but let us not underestimate the double-nature of the wine … remember: beside Jacob there is Esau, too …).

The Figs are seen as symbols for ‚awareness‘, for a certain ‚knowledge through involvement‘ (the fig is traditionally known as the fruit of the ‚Tree of Knowledge of Good and Evil‘); wanting to experience the world intimately, to actually KNOW things in the deepest sense of the word; this is the Sephirah ’netzach‘ and associated with it is ‚Moses‘, as bringing the knowledge of the will of God, enabling us to get into covenant with Him, that is: establish an intimate relationship with our Creator (like the covenant on Mount Sinai is perceived as a ‚wedding‘ between God and His People, and the giving of the Thorah is seen as the acceptance of the ‚marriage-contract‘).

Pomegranates are known as the ornaments on the Highpriest’s (= Aaron’s) garment and on the pillars in front of the Temple, by this especially symbolizing the authority and fruitfulness of the priest as a mediator and of his mediation between creature and Creator through the service of ‚priesthood‘, especially having to handle the ‚qurban‘ of the animals, the approach towards the Eternal through the physical ’shape and form‘ of service, becoming a ‚praise‘ for God (see the Sephirah ‚hod‘); it is associated with ‚activity, action, actual deed‘; in the People of God the ‚compartmentalization‘ of service is compared to the inner shape of the fruit, representing a body, an organism with all the separate organs, connected to one functioning unity, like a ,Holy People' (= the congregation of the Servants of the Eternal, Disciples of Jeshua the Messiah; the so-called ,Body of Christ') should be one unity, but still differentiated internally, too (see here the connection with what was said to planet Jupiter).

The Olive is of course seen as ,the pressed fruit to bring the anointing oil', as the ,foundation' (= ,yesod', the name of the sixth Sephirah) and ,the secret' of the suffering in consequence of the 6th day as a necessity for the anointing on the 8th day (again the word ,yesod', now translated in its other meaning as ,he is a secret'); so the Olive is strongly associated with 'struggle' and the benefit of it (giving the precious oil ONLY by being pressed).

The Date (especially the sweet ,honey' of it) finally is envisioned as symbolizing ,perfection', a tranquility and the promised peace, the 'shalom' to be experienced on the seventh day, if perceived as a world being ,very good', as God Himself sees it according to Genesis 1,31.

Now, the eighth fruit, the Almond, is having only ONE core/seed, too, just like the sixth and seventh (and in contrary to the five first fruits, which all have many seeds inside them); but now with the Almond this one core is actually EDIBLE! It is even the main part to be eaten. So the seed of the Almond is both: by being buried in the ground bringing the new ,tree, bringing new fruit', as well as already BEING fruit in itself. What the other fruits are as a whole, too, but in themselves are split into the two aspects of 'seed (= not really edible, at least not enjoyable)' in the inside,

189

and ‚actual fruit (= edible)‘ enveloping the seed(s) from the outside – and for the Almond now it is ONE, it is not 'split‘ anymore, only split in the 'seed-being-fruit‘ and the protecting, enwrapping, covering peel. The seed, as the core (or the symbolic ‚heart‘), is not 'stoney‘ anymore, we would not hurt our teeth by biting in it, in contrary: it is the essential for our consumption of it!

There are two words for ‚almond‘ in Hebrew: ‚luz‘ and 'shakhed‘. ‚Luz‘ also is the name of the specific place where Jacob dreams of the famous ‚ladder to heaven‘ (see Genesis 28,11ff), and which is thus called ‚Beth El‘ by him, meaning ‚House of God‘. And later this exact spot is becoming the place of the Temple of Jerusalem (according to judaic tradition).

In the mystic perspective, the expression ‚luz‘ beside that also refers to a specific part of the physical body, on which after death the so-called ‚resurrection body‘ will ‚cristallize around‘. It could be seen as the core of our ‚Self‘, of our being as an individual person, that which remains even beyond the corruption of the dead fleshly body, to be revived at another level of existence.

The other word for the almond, 'shakhed‘, is derived from the equally spelled verbal root 'shakhad‘, meaning ‚to hurry, to be vigilent; (to stay) awake; to stand watch‘ (compare this association with ‚fastness‘ to the ‚hind‘ and ‚deer‘, as they have been mentioned in the last part referring to the ‚very fast‘ character of Messiah, and of Salvation, which is experienced).

We now can finally come to the actual hidden planets

190

themselves, after having painted a picture of the crucial transition from the visible world of the seven towards the invisible of the ‚Eight', as representing the primal breakthrough to this invisible, after which the following ‚Nine and Ten (and even until Twelve and Thirteen) will almost ‚flow automatically'.

The 8th planet is simply called ‚the Eighth One' in the Hebrew Astrology. You cannot name it, because we can only name, what is graspable in the time-space-world. But the 8th is something ‚wholly new'. This 8th planet in the horoscope of the individual is the major doorway to the 8th DAY, that is: to ‚Salvation, as being experienced personally, individually'. So it is first and for all pointing to ‚a great joy' for yourself – probably it is indeed the GREATEST possible joy one can experience in this life.

But at some point there will emerge the question: What about all those around you, who are not 'saved' yet? Has not God said: ALL has to be born anew?!

So there will be another ‚judgement', a ‚correction' of the current state, to come, before the ‚child' can be born on the 10th day.

The ‚power of the 8th day and planet' is to be understood for the individual as an infinite possibility to ‚relativize', especially the seemingly ‚bad' things experienced in everyday life in this world: they are not THAT important, only showing a little part of the whole; because it is always about the WHOLE, about life in its totality, and life is always present – because life is eternal. That means, it does not 'start' at some point, but it IS, it does not ‚begin‘ at all, it has no ‚beginning‘, it is here completely in every single moment indeed, always has been, always will be.

To be ‚born anew‘ or reborn, born again, the ‚rebirth‘ means: to be, who you are.

This true character of yourself is to be found on the level of existence represented by this ‚8th planet‘. It brings the attitude of being able to get into contact with eternity, by elevating yourself from the 'seventh' upwards, out of the ‚time-space-world‘ towards the ‚8th day‘, which always was, is and will be accompanying your experience. Remember: you always experience in this life the complex of 6th, 7th and 8th day, only your consciousness is from the 6th day and your body is in the everlasting development of the 7th day (never reaching a final state of perfection here on day 7). Your salvation is present in the 8th day, including all your true longings and desires, all in yourself that draws you towards the future not out of force, but out of attraction, out of the wish to connect, to be in relation(ship) to people and things.

Especially it means the longing for PAST things and happenings to be regained in the (other-worldly) future, too: so much seems to be lost in the passed away times, so many people seem to have not achieved the eternal peace in their lives … what about THEM?! Because you experience your own salvation in the eighth, you worry about all the others.

It is this exact longing, which drives Solomon to the

192

desire to marry the daughter of Pharao: he sees her as representing the 6th day (remember: Egypt is the symbol of this 6th day), that day where the Salvation was not actually realized. So the great King wants the ‚woman of Egypt', that is: the ‚appearance of the passed away times', wants to give her children, here in HIS kingdom of the eighth day.

And in this moment the perishing of this Kingdom is determined, the destruction of the Temple and the split of the Kingdom. ‚Oh, God, that's terrible!!' … we want to scream out here … But only by this means it will be possible to have the return, the comeback of all passed away things and happenings and beings afterwards.

It is the ‚going down into the underworld', into 'she'ol', to experience salvation there and to GIVE salvation there, too. It is the ‚leaving for three days', like the three days, Messiah Jesus was ‚gone', after dying on the cross, before resurrecting.

Although the hidden planets cannot really be described 'separately', by looking at a single one of them detached from the rest of the planets (and especially from the rest of the hidden planets), it nevertheless can be given at least a clue for each of them to be ‚found' in a horoscope, similar to the seven visible planets with their respective unique characteristics, which are ‚found' by seeing or calculating their constellations in the zodiacal signs.

The eighth planet, the especially 'nameless one', is found by looking at the personal name of the individual whose horoscope one is looking into. The 'name' of a being is perceived as much more than a

193

mere purposeful ,marker of distinction' between different social beings and their respective ,data' in all the different collections of information in this civilization nowadays. The NAME is nothing less than the most concentrated description of the innermost essence of the being carrying this name. And to find the (many-layered) meaning of a name (and not only the ,personal name' of our passport is meant here, also every 'nick name' and pseudonym one uses could be integrated in this approach to the ,8th sphere' of a horoscope), there are questions to be taken into account like: How have you got this name? Who gave it to you?

The name of a human being conceals his or her destination and in the name you can see his or her fate.

And sometimes the actual name (from whatever language it may originate ,etymologically') has to be perceived as a Hebrew name, that is: spelled with Hebrew letters and then understood in all its possibilities of translation (which are usually very manifold in the Hebrew language, due to the lack of any true vowel letters determining the consonant letter words in an unambiguos way).

So, as already mentioned when discussing the ,fruit signs' of the Zodiac in the fourth part of this introduction (even with quite some details then), the 'ninth day' is associated with the ,underworld' – and with ,being a womb', too.

Especially here it is experienced that strong connection with, and a longing for the past things. Here you live ,deep inside this past'. And while living ‚there‘, in the darkness the new birth is prepared.

The 9th plague over Egypt (see Exodus 10,21-23) is ‚darkness‘, and on the 10th plague the liberation, the actual exodus happens.

In this darkness, in this womb, the individual gets to know much, which is there inside him/her, of which he/she did not know at all yet. Remember: the 9th letter of the Hebrew Alphabeth is the ‚teth‘, referring to the clay of the potter (which is ‚tiyt‘) and to a ‚womb‘, or to a ‚basket‘, containing something not yet visible. What happens in there is a ‚budding‘, a sprouting of the past things, to become the coming now, but in a ‚resurrected‘ form, not as a mere repetition of the passed away.

As already said, the hidden planets cannot precisely be ‚calculated‘, their message is only to be found out by observing the actual behaviour, by knowing about the inner motivation(s) of the human being whose horoscope is to be interpreted. The ninth planet can be traced in a horoscope by knowing about the longings, wishes and desires of the individual whose horoscope it is. Thus the ninth planet, the second of the hidden ones, could be called the ‚wish planet‘.

The 10th – be it the tenth day or the tenth planet – always is associated with the ‚actual future‘. Of course in some regard all three invisible planets are concerning the future, and not only in a purely timely sense – but the 10th planet is the final breakthrough of that future and of that completely ‚New‘, it is the material realization of the ‚fruit‘, or more mythically

195

spoken: the ,birth of the child out of the womb of this world'.

Thus this tenth planet in the horoscope is displaying the 'structure of the future' of the individual regarding this material realization of the spiritual fruit in one's life. It enables us to see certain ,reactions' in the individual's surrounding world, and these reactions, like 'symptoms', are thereby speaking of this new birth, describing the effects of it, and so indirectly they are telling about the concrete character of this 'new birth'.

Here, in this ,tenth sphere' of existence, ,the coming' already HAS arrived.

The 10th letter of the Hebrew Alphabeth, the ,yod', is the smallest letter of all 22, but by this small letter actually ALL other letters are formed, it is like the fundamental structural element of the script.

The position of the 10th planet in someones horoscope can be identified (to a certain degree) by knowing about the 'state of knowledge' of that individual. That is: about the knowledge itself, its amount and extent, but about the reasons in his/her past life, too, by which he/she happened to be now at this particular state of knowledge: all the coincidences which led one to certain interests, again leading to specific research, or having certain experiences, people one knows, and so on, which brought certain parts of knowledge. And it is not only about what one knows, but about what one NOT knows, too! Sometimes especially a ,deliberate ignorance' regarding certain facts brings the crucial potential for achieving certain things.

196

The possibility of hope in all human existence (ONLY!) exists through these three planets. In the state of hope THAT is already here, what still shall come. If it would not be here already inside the human being, it could not be hoped for, nor expected in any way. This is seen as the ‚proof‘ for the reality even of that, which is still ‚only‘ hoped for.

Therewith, the three planets in their totality are called the ‚planets of hope‘, too.

‚Hope‘, in Hebrew ‚tiqwah‘, is derived from a word ‚qaw‘, meaning ‚proportion; measurement‘. Hope has proportions, is measureable. By looking at the three planets in a horoscope, you could know whether the individual still has hope. If he or she is desperate, the influence of these three planets is missing. He or she then is depressive, knows not an advice what to do (in certain regards).

But even IF the three planets are not having an influence on him/her, there is no actual reason for desperateness, for heaven DOES move, it circulates; so the planets WILL come back, after they ‚made their big round throughout sky‘. Aspects change all the time.

And then after this tenth planet, as already implied above, there are two more planets, making full the ‚Twelve‘, harmonizing thus the planets with the zodiacal signs.

They are called ‚New Sun and New Moon‘, referring to the scripture Isaiah 30,26, which is speaking of the ‚true light‘ of creation being carried in the future by the heavenly bodies Sun and Moon in the New Creation: ‚Moreover the light of the moon shall be as

197

the light of the sun, and the light of the sun shall be sevenfold, as the light of seven days, in the day that the LORD bindeth up the breach of His people, and healeth the stroke of their wound.'

These two planets named ,New Sun and New Moon' not only show and signify hope, but they signify already the REALIZATION of the whole path that is hoped for. Having them influencing the individual means: the human being is tending to realize ,the final things', the ,Ultimate', already here in this life. Then ,the new Sun and the new Moon are here for him/her'.

This 11th and 12th planet are estimated very high in the Ancient Astrology. It is said: a true vision of the future, a clear insight into anything, or a genius idea comes to mind, or manifests itself to the eye of the soul, by means of being ,illuminated by the light of new sun and new moon'.

The 11th and 12th planet are determined by the questions: What is the occupation of the individual, with what kind of everyday activity does he or she take care of his daily needs? And what is the individual looking for, seeking, searching in this world beside his or her employment, what drives the individual's activity of his so-called ,free time' in life, what's one's ,personal mission' in life?

The 10th day, with the 11th and 12th planet as symbols for the light on that 10th day, is in itself a symbol for the becoming of a ,living testimony', witnessing the grace of the Eternal for His servants; it is ,the good side of Leo', in the pictures of the zodiacal signs.

198

With all the questions and answers of the 5 hidden planets of 'name', of ,wish', of ,knowledge', of ,occupation' and of ,mission' taken together, a true ,Wise One' can know even about the standing of the ,thirteenth', too, of the 13th zodiacal sign, as well as of the 13th planet. So for this last rest of an ,absolute incalculateability' in everything, there is no specific detail in itself to be looked at in separation (like to a certain degree this is still the case with the first 5 hidden planets), but only the wholesome, the holistic view on it all, can bring an insight into the 13th.

One rare practice in Judaism has a special connection to the hidden planets: the so-called ,little Yom Kippur', celebrated monthly before each New Moon; or to be more precise: in the last one and a half days of a month, which are seen as representing the ,rest that remains' after the ending of the four full weeks of seven days in one lunar cycle. So it is said: In the last one and a half days of the lunar cycle the ,planets stand very tight', and especially the five ,hidden ones' are here to be sensed. This then is celebrated by a few people in Judaism as a ,little Yom Kippur', to commemorate the moment of dying, similar to the ,big', true Yom Kippur. Typically there is fasting on the little Yom Kippur, like on the regular feast.

In the Talmud of the Jews there is a little story about some poor ,day labourers', and this story in a simple picture is illustrating the basic principle of the so-called ,hidden planets' and their incalculateable influence on an individual destiny. The story goes like this:

A group of day labourers always assembles in the

199

cool shadow of a certain rock formation in the near of their working place, to have their lunch break around noon.

At this point, one of them goes around passing all of them with a sack and everybody throws into the sack what he has brought that day.

One brings a bread, one other a cheese, one other a pomegranate, and so on. With the collected sum of it they then make a nice dish, like the cheese on the bread and the pomegranate as a little dessert for example.

By this method they all share their little food, making it much more diversified and thus more healthy for each of them.

One day one of the workers is having a really tough time: his wife at home is very sick and their children are being already malnutritioned, because for weeks now the money of the family is spent for medicine for the wife. So on this day the husband could not find anything at home which he would be able to share with his co-workers. So he has brought nothing with him to throw into the collecting sack.

Then the lunch break begins, everybody assembles at the shady place near the rocks and one of the guys goes around with the sack. The one worker not having brought anything begins to feel so ashamed, not knowing what to say in the moment, when his co-workers will realize that he has not brought anything for the community to share, and while he starts shaking in fear, not being able to even think straight, the collector approaches him … but the collector already sees from some distance that the poor man has brought nothing to put into the sack, so when he arrives at the man, he does not even leave him the opportunity to say anything, like begging for forgiveness or explaining his unusual behaviour of not bringing anything this day – but he instantly begins praising him and thanking him very loudly and exuberantly, like the poor man had thrown something unexpectably good into the collecting sack. By this nice gesture the poor man is saved from the possible bad reaction of his fellow workers.

And when the man who was collecting the food goes to his place again to sit down and eat, shortly before he arrives at his exact spot, a giant part of the rock falls down from above and crushes the whole place there. Luckily, the man was still far enough away to not even get hurt. Would he had arrived already and sat down, the piece of the rock would have crushed him to death for sure.

Then it is explained from an astrological point of view:

From the beginning of creation this piece of the rock was destined to fall down on that man to kill him on that exact day. Only his spontaneous decision, to save his co-worker from being ridiculed or hated for bringing nothing to the shared lunch meal, has stopped this fixed destiny from happening. Because just through the time spent speaking in great and long words about the exquisiteness of the food-donation of the poor man, he came a little bit later back to his own spot under the rock, so that the piece of stone already has fallen down, before he actually arrived and sat down. A ‚babylonian' horoscope would have not been able to take into account this sudden turn of

201

his destiny, because it would have ignored the hidden planets, in this case maybe especially the planet defined by the 'name', representing the merciful character of that man with the collecting sack, also the planet defined by his ‚knowing' of the lack of anything brought by the poor man, and the planet of his ‚wish' to not have the poor man hated by his co-workers, and so on.

So this taking into account of the ‚hidden planets' is one major factor for the great difference between Hebrew and Babylonian mode of Astrology.

Another very important difference to the babylonian approach to an individual's horoscope also shall be mentioned briefly: In the Hebrew method, the horoscope of the birthday (or any other day to be looked into) can be (and should be) viewed also with regard to certain other (‚mythically relevant') days of the respective (biblical) year. That means for example: For the horoscope of the fifth day of the 10th month (called ‚Tevet', the month of Capricorn) in the biblical year number 5754, it would be looked into the horoscopes of certain other dates around this particular date of birth. Especially the biblical Feast Days would be taken into account here: New Year (or ‚Yom Teruah', on the New Moon of Libra), Jom Kippur (on the 10th day of Libra), Sukkoth (from Full Moon of Libra until waning Half Moon of Libra), Pessach (including the following week of ‚Matzoth' and the ‚day of the firstfruits offering', called ‚Bikkurim'; from Full Moon of Aries until waning Half Moon of Aries) and Shavuoth (or ‚Pentecost', meaning ‚fifty' in greek, so ‚the feast of the fifty', referring to the 50th day, or to the 'seven times seven

202

weeks' counted from the firstfruits offering on, after which this feast is celebrated; always in the beginning of the month of Gemini, in the example of a birth on the fifth of Capricorn in 5754 Shavuoth would be precisely on the fifth of Gemini).

Beside these biblically established feast days, there are other potentially important special days, too, to be taken into account, which can be found in the Bible itself or in the Hebrew tradition concerning it. For instance the date of the beginning of the great flood (17th day of 2nd month, shortly after Full Moon of Taurus), the day of the first erection of the ,mishkhan', the ,tabernacle of the congregation' (1st day of 2nd month, New Moon of Taurus), the Day of the Fall of Jerusalem (17th day of the 4th month, shortly after Full Moon of Cancer), the Day of the Destruction of the Temple (9th day of the fifth month, shortly after waxing Half Moon of Leo), the so-called ,New Year of the Trees' (Full Moon of Aquarius), the ,Feast of Channukah' (25th day of Sagittarius till 3rd day of Capricorn), the ,Feast of Purim' (14th and 15th day, that is around Full Moon of Pisces).

It is then looked which planets of the birthday horoscope are being in conjunction, opposition and/or square to the dates of these several biblically relevant happenings in the horoscope, to determine by this the influence of the happenings of these days ,in the mythical realm' (which can be read out of the biblical narratives) on the individual, and in which specific way these influences are reaching the individual (that is: on what ,level of existence', on which ,Sephirah', that is: by which of the planets the

203

influence is primarily experienced, and in which zodiacal sign or signs beside the one of the biblical happening itself it is occuring, etc.).

Summarizing this sixth part of the introduction to Hebrew Astrology we can state: By the ‚hidden planets‘ and the 13th zodiacal sign a tremendously great revolution of the visible horoscope can be realized – and literally EVERY single detail of the purely ‚babylonian‘ horoscope, the part of a horoscope only dealing with the visible signs and planets, can be relativized by what can be called ‚the human factor‘ or ‚human freedom of will‘ or just: relativized by the experienceable ‚Assistance of the Eternal‘, by a ‚divine grace, granted to the individual‘.

There is indeed a Hebrew expression in Judaism, which illustrates this consciousness of the true People of God ’not being slaves to the stars‘; it is the expression usually translated as ‚idolators‘: ‚Akum‘, or more precisely to be spelled ‚A-K-U-M‘, because it is an acronym for the words ‚Abed Kokhavim U Mazloth‘, which mean ’servant of stars and constellations‘. In everyday language of modern day profane jews it is just used as a term to say ‚idol worshipper‘, or even more unprecise as simply referring to any ‚infidel‘ or to a ‚heathen‘. But in its original sense it means something very specific: It refers to any kind of superstition, that outer circumstances determine your character and destiny FOR GOOD, unchangeably. Yes, they DO influence you, as long as you are still walking in the flesh of your body on this Earth; but there always will be the freedom of your choices and especially what is expressed in the horoscope as the ‚hidden planets‘ and the 13th of the zodiacal signs.

If you do not know the particular human being the horoscope you are looking at is based on, you should not interpret it at all. Only in the ‚flowing to and fro‘ of the words and feelings, while speaking about the constellations of the horoscope, there will be the possibility to get a glimpse into the ‚hidden planets‘, too. And only with them there can be a true interpretation, a living understanding of the destiny and its potential. Without the hidden ones, the horoscope stays a dead prognosis with statistical significance – but without any taking into account ‚the human factor‘, that, which is part of what makes Mankind ‚in the resemblance of the Eternal‘, being able to choose in every new moment anew, ‚from which tree we want to eat‘.

Out of the hidden sphere originates all the freedom of Mankind, of the individual.

And especially out of the thirteenth. The 8th already brings the impulse for the following 9th, 10th, 11th, 12th and then for the 13th, so the 8th is already the implication of the 13th, 8 and 13 are tightly connected, like the 8th day of the seven-day-week and the 13th moon of the 12-month-year: it is that incalculateable rest of everything appearing, which escapes our definite estimation and understanding. From here we get our possibility for love, too, for all intimacy in the relation to each other, as well as to ‚the world as a whole‘, and to anything specific in it. All ‚warmth of the soul‘ in the human being stems from here.

In probably every ‚religion‘ there is some kind of envisioning of the so-called ‚end of days‘, a cosmic ‚End Times‘, when the world (as we know it) will cease to exist for good. In the Hebrew language the expression for this ‚end of days‘ would be ‚ketz ha-yamim‘ (literally meaning ‚peak of the days‘, or even ‚thorn of the days‘; and the word ‚days‘ is spelled exactly in the same way like the word for ‚oceans, seas‘ would be spelled – so here we see the strong connection again between the concepts of ‚time‘ and of ‚water‘ in the Hebrew mind).

Now, in the mystic Wisdom there is the custom to change the last letter of that expression from a Mem to a Nun, from a ‚m‘ to a ’n‘, making it ‚ketz ha-yamin‘, literally meaning ‚peak/thorn of the right (hand side)‘. It represents ‚the Mem being replaced by the Nun‘, ‚the 50 instead of the 40‘. This little ‚play on words‘ is supposed to stress the fact that in the true and actual ‚End of Days‘ there is not only a linear end of time, but it is the reaching of a totally new level, a level which is just ‚beyond our time‘ – indeed ‚the Fifty‘, as the crucial step even beyond the ‚fulfillment‘ of the (world of the) Seven (the 7×7, the 49).

206

The Wise One and the Serpent at his Daughter's Wedding

To conclude this introduction with this seventh and last part, we want to encounter a little tale, which is found in the Hebrew tradition, and which can be read as an illustration of the application of astrological knowledge by a truly ‚Wise One'.

In the tradition there are several slightly different accounts of that certain story which elaborates on an ‚astrological component' to an episode in the life of the famous jewish teacher and Wise One with the name Aqiba Ben Yoseph. That story tells about the wedding of Aqibas daughter.

But to be able to grasp all depths of the story we firstly should get a little bit familiar with the legendary ‚currucilum vitae' of this famous Wise One Aqiba. Although this Aqiba indeed has existed somewhen around 2000 years ago as an actual person, for our purpose here the focus is not at all about the question what were the actual happenings of his life; but we rather look into the rich amount of legends concerning his person, because these legends especially illustrate certain spiritual concepts – and in the following it will be about this one specific legend illustrating the spiritual concept of the ‚hidden planets' and their vital importance in a horoscope, and, in preparation for this main story, it will be also about some other episodes in Aqiba's life, which ‚made him ready' to finally perform his wisdom regarding that decisive horoscope.

Let us first introduce Aqiba's first wife, known as Rachel, who is the mother of the daughter that is going to marry in the main plot of the story.

This Rachel was the daughter of a rich man of Jerusalem, a certain Kalba Sh'vua (aramaic for ‚Dog of the Seven' or ‚Dog of the Oath'). Aqiba has been growing up as a very poor man, at some point becoming a servant at the house of this rich Aramean named Kalba Sh'vua, working for him as a shepherd until he is fourty years of age. Up to this point of his life Aqiba was illiterate, uneducated and without any hopeful future expectations.

Nevertheless the beautiful Daughter of Kalba Sh'vua, Rachel (a name meaning 'sheep; mother sheep'), fell in love with that poor, uneducated shepherd Aqiba, in whom she saw much more than what the rest of the world would see in him. Of course her father was not very pleased with the idea, that his daughter is going to marry a poor illiterate shepherd … and when she still kept holding fast to this wish, even after her father disagreed to it, Kalba Sh'vua felt to be obliged to drive her (and with her Aqiba, too) away without any possession.

So Aqiba and Rachel are now both poor, only having each other, and finally get married.

Motivated by his dear wife, Aqiba eventually decides to become educated. Rachel strongly encourages him in this question, even knowing that he will have to leave her for a long time to do so. This is the reason, why in Judaism this wife of Aqiba is seen as a prototype of a ‚good wife', encouraging and supporting her husband to study the recommendations of the Eternal.

Aqiba then indeed is gone studying for 22 long years.

And he comes back with 22.000 students. He arrives at the house of his wife, and before being seen by her, he is listening to a conversation between her and a neighbour woman, who is making fun of her, saying: ‚Your husband is gone for twentytwo years now … he will never come back, he has left you! Don't you get it?!‘ But Aqiba's wife responds: ‚He said to me that he is going to be back as soon as he has learned what he has to learn. So even if he is gone for another seven years, I will be waiting for him in patience!‘ And Aqiba, hearing this, decides to not show himself to her at this point already, but leaves the country again and studies for another seven years, then coming back with even much more students being amazed by his wisdom and knowledge. His two most famous students are later known by the names of Me'iyr (which means ‚illuminating one‘) and Shim'on Bar Yochai (who is the legendary founder of the mystical tradition of the Kabbalah, especially famous as the author of the book called ‚Zohar‘, a word meaning 'splendour, radiation‘).

So after 29 years of studying Aqiba arrives back in the region of his origin. And he coincidentally meets his old employer, the father of his wife Rachel, Kalba Sh'vua. Of course Kalba Sh'vua does not recognize Aqiba after all these years and after his transformation from a poor illiterate shepherd to a highly honoured Wise One with thousands of own students. And seeing his great wisdom, he asks Aqiba for an advice concerning his long gone away daughter, whom he ‚had to drive out and dispossess‘ 29 years ago, because she wanted to marry someone much ‚below her value‘, that very uneducated shepherd. Aqiba asks Kalba Sh'vua: ‚Well, would you have let her marry him, if he would have promised to start studying the Word of God?' And he responds: ,Yes, of course, if that shepherd only would have learned to recite the Shema-prayer or to sing one single Psalm – I instantly would have allowed the marriage!'

Hearing this answer, seeing the true longing of the father to reunite with his daughter, Aqiba reveals to him that HE is that poor illiterate shepherd, having studied the Word of God for 29 years now. Kalba Sh'vua is very happy to hear that, finally meets his daughter again, everybody is happy and Kalba Sh'vua even gives half of his rich possessions to Aqiba and Rachel.

It is told that Aqiba was of an age of forty years when he married the daughter of Kalba Sh'vua and left his house with her; so he would have been 69 when he arrived back after his studying as the great Wise One, one 'step ahead' to the ,Seventy', representing the effectual ,everything' in this ,world of the seven'. And now it is said: with 80 years Aqiba married a second wife (compare this to the 'split of the kingdom', which is necessarily happening on the end of the ,8th day'; for this topic see part 3 again: the paragraph concerning the sign of Scorpio).

Aqiba's second wife is known as ,the beautiful Roman woman'. She used to be the wife of a certain Roman named Turnus Rufus (sometimes called ,Tyrannus Rufus', later becoming the one responsible for Aqiba being killed as a martyr), who back then was the provincial governor of the Roman occupied Judean region called Palastine; so he was the major representative of the Roman Caesar in this area. And

210

this Turnus Rufus used to have regular discussions with Aqiba about all kinds of questions of philosophy, always trying to ,make Aqiba a good Roman' by convincing him with ,logical arguments'. But, as to be expected, he always fails to achieve anything in this regard, he always ,loses' in the discussions, even has to agree regularly to the standpoint of Aqiba in the end, having his own arguments turned around against himself by the wisdom and the rethorical talent of Aqiba.

Regularly, after Turnus Rufus has lost another one of his arguments with Aqiba, the Roman governor comes home to his wife and complains to her about that cracked, cunning Jew, who always achieves to twist around his thorough Roman philosophemes and turns them to become weapons against himself instead …

And at one of these occasions one night, his wife ultimately is effectually annoyed by this custom of having regularly to listen to the monotonous complaints of her husband for having lost again. So she decides to try it now herself, ,on her way', to convince Aqiba of the assumed superiority of their Roman philosophy. That means: She wants to seduce Aqiba with her ,female charm'.

And as already mentioned, this wife of Turnus Rufus is said to be very beautiful; indeed so beautiful that every man who sees her appearance instantly forgets everything else and only wants to possess HER from then on.

Now the story tells: when this Roman woman comes to Aqiba to seduce him, he is behaving in a very strange manner:

Aqiba spits out, then he weeps, and then he laughs. Of course the woman asks, what the meaning of this behaviour is … and Aqiba responds: I spat out, because this beauty of yours is mere flesh that seduces. I then cried, because this beauty of yours, which IS existing indeed as such – I cannot deny that – is going to corrupt and disappear with time. But why I still was laughing in the end, I cannot explain to you in a sentence.

Now of course the Roman woman is very excited and wants to know exhaustingly, why exactly there will be a reason to laugh for Aqiba in the end nevertheless …

And now Aqiba goes into all the depths of his understanding of creation and Mankind's journey through this world, and explains her in a many hour long teaching throughout the whole night, why there will still be a reason to be happy in the end, despite of the corruption of all fleshly beauty, which in the first place is not avoidable in this world of time and space.

Roughly the final essence of Aqiba's answer could be sketched out as: ,Even for YOU there exists ,repentance', a ,returning home', wherein that which is flowing away with time, like your fleshly beauty, will be reconnected with the Eternal Source, and the human being thereby will be able to know his or her life in the Eternal, his own LIVING in the Eternal, and he or she will be experiencing it already now, ,during the course of time' in this material world.' And by means of this, it is told, that beautiful Roman

212

woman becomes Aqiba's second wife.

And when marrying for a second time, for Aqiba begins his ‚journey towards Paradise', of which there are several accounts in the tradition. We remember that this second marriage of him occurs when Aqiba is 80 years old. And the whole span of his life is said to have been 120 years. So this point where he is 80 years of age marks the spot of transition ‚from the 2 to the 1' in his life experience, from the ‚2 times 40 years' to the ‚1 times 40 years'.

And to be more precise concerning his ‚famous journey towards Paradise': Out of the four Wise Ones who started that journey towards Paradise together, Aqiba is the only one that actually RETURNED (at good health) from the adventure of getting through ‚the 7 heavens, each having 7 halls' on the pathway to Paradise …

Aqiba's three companions on the journey are named Shim'on Ben Zoma, Shim'on Ben Azzai and Elisha Ben Abuyah (mostly only referred to as ‚the other one').

The talmudic account of the happenings is very short and goes like this (see for example Talmud Bavli; Chagigah 14b):

Four entered the Paradise. They were Ben Azzai, Ben Zoma, ‚the Other One' and Aqiba. Aqiba said to them, ‚When you come to the place of pure marble stones, do not say, ‚Water! Water!' for it is said, ‚He who speaks untruths shall not stand before My eyes' (see Psalms 101,7)'. Ben Azzai gazed and died. Regarding him the verse states, ‚Precious in the eyes of God is the death of His pious ones' (Psalms

213

116,15). Ben Zoma gazed and was harmed. Regarding him the verse states, ‚Did you find honey? Eat only as much as you need, lest you be overfilled and vomit it‘ (Proverbs 25,16). The ‚Other One‘ cut down the plantings. Regarding him the verse states, ‚Do not let your mouth bring your flesh to sin, and do not say before the angel that it is an error; why should God become angry at your voice, and ruin the work of your hands‘ (Ecclesiastes 5,5). Aqiba entered in peace and left in peace. Regarding him the verse states, ‚Draw me, let us run after you, the King has brought me into His chambers‘ (Song of Solomon 1,4).

The further elaborations on this short story explain it in different respects. One of them is given by the popular interpreter Sh'lomoh Yitzchaki and states that Shim'on Ben Azzai ‚dies after the half of his days‘ (often understood as meaning, that he only got to ‚know one of the two sides of life‘, never learning about the divine blessings being present inside HIMSELF, too, as well as that the whole world is present inside himself), Shim'on Ben Zoma ‚loses his sanity‘ (and becomes a little bit 'self-opinionated‘, arrogant – to not call it ‚megalomaniac‘ …), and Elisha Ben Abuyah ‚becomes a mocker‘, a ‚renegade and apostate‘ (which is the reason why he is typically only referred to as ‚the other one‘ afterwards, not giving him the honor of mentioning him by name).

So only Aqiba survives their adventure without any harm to his soul. This is explained by Friedrich Weinreb with the fact that Aqiba as the only one of the four did not skip any of the ‚four stages‘ necessary to enter the Paradise properly.

214

These four stages are said to be:

Firstly you learn to see the world how it really is.

Secondly you experience the world in the Word (of God).

Thirdly you reenact all that you have learned by now during the first two stages, but now experiencing it inside yourself, inside your own soul.

In the fourth stage then, an angel is sent to you, from now on accompanying you during your everyday life, showing you the way towards Paradise INSIDE this world and inside your life in this world.

In the end you arrive at a fountain, where two women are standing. And as always in the mythical language, a ‚woman' represents an ‚appearance', especially of the world, but of any individual being or happening, too (like for example the ‚happening' of Salvation …).

For Akiva here the two women are his two wives: the one who sacrificed herself (respectively her wealthy inheritance) for him, the other one who was trying to seduce him.

And at some point you will realize that the two women actually are ONE. That is the moment, when the Gates of Paradise open for you and you see yourself finally in the image of God, in the resemblance of the Eternal, how you originally were created to be from the beginning of All.

In a way, the three first stages on the path towards Paradise are represented in the female, the male and the fruit signs of the Zodiac, too.

215

When Aqiba is asked afterwards, what was it like, to approach Paradise more and more on his journey towards it, he responds: ,It began with a lot of conversations with a lot of people. Really, so many conversations, all the time getting more and more, that I already believed, there will never be an end to these conversations. But then, after a long time, these conversations got more and more focused to certain topics, more and more limited to certain people I conversed with. And then, from some point on, I was only talking to one person about one topic, and nothing else any more. And in the end ... I was standing in front of a mirror, realizing that it was all along only me myself I was talking to during my whole life. That's when I realized what it truly means, to be created in the image of God. From now on, everytime I am thinking about postponing anything or pushing away responsibility for anything, two questions arise in my mind: When, if not now? And: Who, if not you?'

Shim'on Ben Azzai, the one of the four who is ,dying at the half of his days', is credited in the jewish tradition for having proclaimed to the public the last adding of books to the Hebrew part of the Bible, namely the book of ,Ecclesiastes' and the ,Song of Solomon'. Beside this he is the one Aqiba's daughter is betrothed to for a long time before finally marrying her (although many sources deny this final marriage – but for telling our story here it is helpful to assume that this marriage happened in the end ...).

Although he eventually dies ,at the half of his days' due to his failure to go through ALL the stages on his way to Paradise (because he is skipping the stage of

216

reenacting the two first stages inside his own soul: the knowledge how the world really is and the experience of the world in the Word of God – he only gets to know the truth as an outer reality and is already too overwhelmed by that), Ben Azzai still is remembered as an especially ‚pious one', having died by taking a glance at the splendour of the Eternal One, thereby ‚dying the death of His saints'.

Shim'on Ben Zoma seems to have skipped the stage of experiencing the whole world as existing (only) INSIDE the Word of God, when he was on his way towards Paradise. That is why he ‚got mad' when beholding the splendor of God as the same as his own splendor, for being himself created in the resemblance of the Eternal – but not being able to differentiate effectually ‚between the original and the mere image in the mirror', so to speak.

He is characterized in the Talmud by looking at a 'scholar of the Scriptures' as the ‚crown of creation' – a thought, which led him to a certain over-estimation of his own person. This is illustrated for instance by the following episode that is told about him (Tosefta, Bereshith 6,2; Bereshith 58a):

Ben Zoma, seeing the crowds on the Temple mount, said, ‚Blessed be He who created all these to attend to my needs. How much had Adam to weary himself with! Not a mouthful could he taste before he plowed and sowed, and cut and bound sheaves, and threshed and winnowed and sifted the grain, and ground and sifted the flour, and kneaded and baked, and then he ate; but I get up in the morning and find all this ready before me. How much had Adam to weary himself with! Not a shirt could he put on before he sheared and washed the wool, and hatcheled and dyed and spun and wove and sewed, and then he clothed himself; but I rise in the morning and find all this ready before me. How many trades are anxiously busy early in the morning; and I rise and find all these things before me!'

Elisha Ben Abuyah did not want to learn about the real world how she really is, as it would have been the appropriate first stage of the journey to Paradise – he wanted to only find it all in studying the Word of God. That is why he ultimately got destroyed by the real world: One day he witnessed the death of a young boy falling from a tree and breaking his neck: The father of that boy had asked his son to climb on the tree to get the eggs from a nest, but to let the mother bird fly away, just like the Bible recommends it. The boy listened to his father and thus not only kept the recommendation concerning the eggs and the mother bird, but also the so-called ‚fifth commandment‘ of the Ten Words, to ‚honour father and mother‘. And both biblical recommendations explicitly go with the motivating explanation, to do it 'so that your days will be prolonged‘ (see Exodus 20,12 and Deuteronomy 22,7). And still the boy died at such a young age through having this terrible accident.

Elisha Ben Abuyah was not able to integrate this experience into his understanding of the greatness of God. He could not grasp this apparent contradiction between his own deep insight into the essence of all existence which he gained through his ‚journey to Paradise‘ (= deepest ‚esoteric insights‘) on the one side and the shockingly brutal reality on the other side, because he never learned to see the world how she really is, only knowing the world as a harmonic creation of the Eternal, as existing inside the Word of God, and by having experienced this world inside himself, inside his own soul. So he could not accept the ‚outer world' around him as being indeed ‚very good', as God Himself has stated – and so Elisha Ben Abuyah began desacrating the Sabbath, testifying by this, that this ‚world of the seventh day' in his eyes is NOT ‚very good', that we should NOT rest in her, and NOT let her be how she is …

We now want to focus on a kabbalistic perspective on the journey to Paradise, and we will be approaching this perspective with the knowledge of the mythical symbolism already established in the past six parts of this introduction. Firstly, in the famous kabbalistic book named ‚Zohar' (Hebrew for 'splendour') there is an additional notice concerning the already cited short talmudic account of the story, which goes like the following (see Zohar I, 26b; Tikkunei Zohar, Tikkun 40):

The ancient Saba (an old man) stood up and said (to Shim'on Bar Yochai, the legendary author of the Zohar, and one of the two most famous students of Aqiba), ‚Teacher, Teacher! What is the meaning of what Aqiba said to his students, ‚When you come to the place of pure marble stones, do not say ‚Water! Water!' lest you place yourselves in danger, for it is said, ‚He who speaks untruths shall not stand before My eyes."

But it is written, ‚There shall be a firmament between the waters and it shall separate between water (above the firmament) and water (below the firmament)'

(Genesis 1,6).

Since the Torah describes the division of the waters in to upper and lower, why should it be problematic to mention this division? Furthermore, since there are upper and lower waters why did Aqiba warn them, ,do not say, ,Water! Water!"

The Holy Lamp (in Aramaic ,botzina kadisha', a title of honour for Shim'on bar Yochai, since he – like being a Lamp himself – has given the ,Splendour', that is: the ,Zohar', being its author) replied, ,Saba, it is proper that you reveal this secret that the Chevraya (literally ,fellowship'; Shim'on's circle of disciples) have not grasped clearly.'

The ancient Saba answered, ,Teacher, Teacher, Holy Lamp. Surely the pure marble stones are the letter ,yod' – one the upper ,yod' of the letter ,aleph', and one the lower ,yod' of the letter ,aleph'. Here there is no spiritual impurity, only pure marble stones, so there is no separation between one water and the other; they form a single unity from the aspect of the Tree of Life, which is the ,waw' in the midst of the letter ,aleph'. In this regard it states, ,and if he take of the Tree of Life (and eat and live forever)' (Genesis 3,22)…

The last three sentences cited refer to the shape of the letter ,aleph', the first letter of the Hebrew Alphabeth with the numeric value of 1 (see part two of this introduction): it is built up of one yod in the upper right, one yod in the lower left and a waw slightly diagonal between them both, by this, equally separating them as connecting them. So together these three components of the written, the appearing

220

shape of the Aleph are having the numeric value of 26 (yod + yod + waw = 10 + 10 + 6 = 26), just as the ‚ineffable name of God‘, the so-called ‚Tetragrammaton‘, the ‚four-letter-name‘ Y-H-W-H (10 + 5 + 6 + 5 = 26).

Especially one kabbalistic teacher of the 16th century (Moses Ben Jacob Cordovero) elaborates on this Zohar-account in a way roughly described in the following (based on his major work ‚Pardes Rimonim‘, see therein Sha'ar Arachei Ha-Kinuim; ‚mayim‘):

God, as the Eternal One, is described as ‚the beginning and the end‘ (see for instance Isaiah 44,6; 48,12; Revelation 1,17).

This can be illustrated in the very first letter of the Hebrew Alphabeth: The upper yod of the shape of the letter aleph is perceived as representing the ‚beginning‘, and especially as the first letter of the ‚ineffable name of the Eternal‘, the ‚Tetragrammaton‘ (YHWH); the lower yod is perceived as representing the ‚end‘, and especially as the last letter of the specific divine name which in the tradition is usually used as a substitute to be pronounced instead of the ‚ineffable name‘, ‚Adonay‘ (spelled Aleph-Daleth-Nun-Yod).

So the two yods are representing the ‚inner‘ and ‚outer‘ aspect of God, the ‚male‘ and ‚female‘, which are separated and connected by the diagonal waw between them. This shape is also mirrored in creation itself, where the ‚upper waters‘ are 'separated‘ from the ‚lower waters‘ by the ‚firmament‘ – and only from a divine perspective they are still

CONNECTED through the firmament, and NOT separated.

So depending on the point of view, it can be ‚true' to speak of the ‚two waters' (when looked at the firmament from ‚down here', from out of the ‚lower waters'), or it can be ‚untrue' to look at them as separate, because they still form a harmonic unity (when looked at our world of the ‚lower waters' from above, from the perspective of the heavenly ‚upper waters').

And now we can look again at the scheme of the Sephiroth, this time taking into account the three ‚upper Sephiroth', too:

$$-I-$$
$$III-II$$
$$2-1$$
$$-3-$$
$$5-4$$
$$-6-$$
$$-7-$$

The unity of the upper three Sephiroth is referred to as the ‚realm of Being', while below these three our world of the seven Sephiroth is the ‚realm of Becoming'. Especially the very lowest Sephirah, called malkhuth, represents our world of the seventh day (as already explained in part 3 and 5 of this introduction). The six Sephiroth from ‚chesed' to ‚yesod' (1 to 6), representing the first six days of creation week, are identified with the original state of being of the ‚Son of Man‘ in the resemblance of God, as connecting the Heavens and the Earth (see part 3 again, the paragraph concerning the sign of Virgo), like ‚an image of God on the firmament‘ (see part 4, especially the paragraph concerning the sign of Capricorn) connecting the ‚two waters‘ – it is primordial Mankind, before being ’shattered into pieces‘ through the so-called ‚Fall of Mankind‘, which brought us into the ’seventh day‘, into the Sephirah malkhuth, where now all the seven lower Sephiroth concentrate together as our physical reality.

The ‚realm of Being‘ is called ‚yesh‘ in the Hebrew (meaning ‚existence; to be‘; spelled with the letters yod and shin). The lowest Sephirah of malkhuth in relation to these upper three is called ’shay‘ (meaning ‚present, gift‘; spelled with the letters shin and yod), because it represents the ‚kingdom‘ and the ‚kingship‘ which is destined to be given to Mankind by the Eternal One, when finally this world is being reconnected to its heavenly origin through the repentance of Mankind.

These two words ’shay‘ and ‚yesh‘, below and above, are connected by the ’six‘, by the original (and final) form of the ‚Son of Man‘ as created on the sixth day, which is (still/again) equal to the ‚Son of God‘, in perfect resemblance of the Heavenly Father. So the ’six‘ (which is the numeric value of the sixth letter Waw, the ’nail‘, see again the beginning of part 2 and the sign of Virgo in part 3) is the diagonal separation and connection of the ‚yod in the beginning‘ and the ‚yod in the end‘, the ‚yesh‘ and the ’shay‘, the ineffable, internal ‚YHWH‘ and the pronounceable, external ‚Adonay‘ – and again we see the shape of the very first letter of the Hebrew Alphabeth, the two yods being mirrored by the diagonal waw, forming the aleph.

Now, the two words 'shay' and ,yesh' being connected to become a single unity, will form the word spelled shin-yod-shin, then pronounced 'shayish'. And this Hebrew word means ,marble'.

So in the ,marble stones' of the Paradise we find the unity of the upper and lower, and it would be an ,untruth' to speak of ,two distinct' beings (,Water! Water!') from this point of view. That is the reason, why Aqiba tried to warn his fellow travelers with the enigmatic words: ,Do not say ,Water! Water!' when coming to the place of pure marble stones.'

Let us now finally look at the story of the wedding of Aqiba's daughter. She is the daughter from his first wife, from Rachel, and some accounts of the story add that she is Aqiba's only daughter. And because her Fiancée, Ben Azzai, lets her wait for him very, very long, while he is studying the Bible, she has a similar destiny as her mother, who also had to wait for many years for Aqiba, while he was studying far away.

In the weeks before the wedding Aqiba once speaks to a babylonian friend who is an astrologer, a 'stargazer'. He tells Aqiba with shy bitterness in his voice, that he has looked into the stars with regard to the coming wedding – and while doing so he has unfortunately found out that Aqiba's daughter is going to be deathly bit by a snake exactly on her wedding day! Aqiba lets his babylonian friend show him the exact horoscope and recalculates all the constellations … and yes, his friend seems to be right, there are no errors in the calculation: his beloved daughter's stars are pointing to a sure death on her wedding day by a bite of a snake!

Aqiba, in spite of the seemingly unavoidable death of his daughter, keeps on preparing the feast. He does not tell his daughter anything about her horoscope. Only, he tries to take all possible precautions to prevent a snake attack on her: He positions specifically instructed watchers on every possible entrance to the place of festivities, he lets search through all the interiour for snakes the whole day before the wedding, and he organizes a substantial amount of any possible antidote against snake venom that he can get.

Then the wedding begins and it seems that everything is going to be fine.

At some point the bride notices that outside at the entrance of the house a beggar is standing, looking in shyness into the place with all the joyously celebrating folk, not daring to raise his voice to ask anyone inside for a small charity. As Aqiba's daughter becomes aware of him, she leaves her place of honour, unnoticed by the rest of the guests, and walks through the celebrating masses towards the beggar standing at the entrance. She asks him in, takes his garment and hangs it on one of the last arrows available in the quiver (it was a custom back then to leave a soft area in the wall of loam near the entrance of a house, so one could stick an arrow into the wall to hang a garment over it), and she gives him to eat of her own meal.

When the wedding finally has ended, it is getting clear: no one got hurt! Now Aqiba finally tells his daughter about the treatening fate described by the horoscope of her, and she is asked whether she did anything special during the night of the wedding. But she cannot remember anything noteworthy. When she is asked to try to recall the entire evening and tell what she has been doing from hour to hour, she also mentions the episode with the beggar. And Aqiba instantly assumes in this specific occurence the reason for the unexpected rescue of his beloved daughter.

So he and some equally interested guests ask from the bride, where exactly she has hung the beggar's garment, after she let him in. She shows them the arrow – and when they draw it out of the wall, it becomes apparent: the arrow stuck into the wall by Aqiba's daughter coincidentally has pierced through the head of a snake that was hiding in the wall!

It is said: that snake was destined to be lurking there in the wall from the beginning of whole creation, just to bite the daughter of Aqiba on that very day, and the bite should have been deathly. She only survives, because she did something ‚good‘, caring about the beggar, something, which nobody could have possibly expected from her to do out of a purely rational, ‚human‘ perspective.

Aqiba's babylonian friend who calculated the horoscope which now proved to be erroneous, asks Aqiba: How did you know that this is going to happen?

Aqibas explanation to his friend then is something

226

like this: Since he knew the ‚hidden planets' of his beloved daughter, he could see in the calculated horoscope presented by the babylonian stargazer more than the Babylonian himself could see. And then Aqiba shows to his friend all the hidden planets in the horoscope, by this, opening him the eyes for what Aqiba, as a ‚Wise One', has been seeing all along.

Friedrich Weinreb retells the explaining speech of Aqiba with the following words:

‚She wanted to marry. It also was the man she was longing for. I myself know from my own destiny, how it is if you want to marry but cannot. If you want to marry, then it means that you have a great desire for the other extreme; and only this exact desire can divest the Serpent of its power.

Where in the Bible does the Serpent appear? It appears, where Man and Woman are in Paradise, and we say that the Serpent seduces the Woman. In this situation the Serpent has power, because there is only a natural, an instinctive connection between Man and Woman, so to speak. But if there is present the desire for a real unification, for marriage, for true connection … then the Serpent, the snake is powerless. That's what I knew already from the very name of my daughter!'

The name of Aqiba's daughter is Nechamah, the female variant of Menachem, with the meaning of ‚consoler, comforter; solace'. And where there is solace, you survive.

And beside her name, Aqiba knew the wishes and the longings of his daughter, too (and of course also her

227

state of knowledge, her occupation, and her ‚mission'). He knew, she will be quick to take care of any poor man begging for help, even without actual words being spoken, and especially, when there is noone else to take care of him.

So, as already mentioned in the explanation of Aqiba speaking to his babylonian friend, there is a crucial meaning of this story for the whole world, if understood not only as a random tale, but as the deep symbol this legend actually embodies:

It is then representing the happenings in the Garden of the beginning: showing the world ‚on her wedding day', when she is about to celebrate the communion with her creator, represented in ‚the crown of creation', Mankind, taking of the fruit of the Tree of Life.

But then this world on the edge of the Holy Wedding is being ‚bit by the snake'. And indeed: the ‚horoscope' of this world, represented by the daughter of Aqiba, is showing clearly that this deathly snake bite HAS to happen. But still, this determination of destiny is only true as the 'norm', ‚in general' … it is NOT necessarily true for the specific case of the single human being, in contrary: every one of us has the chance to be (again) in the image of God and now STAY like that, without being bit by the snake and by this, being made to ‚fall short from the original glory', becoming ‚captive to Death'.

Here again we see: it is only the distinction made by the question whether we are taking into account the ‚hidden planets' of our life – or not, rather prefering

228

to remain a mere 'statistical fact', blurring into an anonymous mass, without any true individuality of ourselves.

But if we have accepted, that any calculateable, ‚babylonian‘ approach to our destiny is only concerning the outer, the superficial side of existence, which always can be overcome by the inner ambition of a liberated human will … then this Hebrew Astrology, which has been introduced during the last 60.000 words, can give us the means and methods to handle our destiny in a way, worthy of us, as the ‚Crown of Creation‘, with every one of us as a messenger of the Eternal, being created in the resemblance of God and destined to bear witness to this fact of our existence.

Hallelu Jah!

*Dedicated to the Unique Angel delivering
me this Message in Her Smashing Impact –
with all the accompanying Up's and Down's
... thereby teaching me to thank God for
Life ,at its Fullest', that is: for Life as one
WHOLE.*

...

Selah!